SPIRITS ALONG THE COLUMBIA RIVER

SPIRITS ALONG THE COLUMBIA RIVER

IRA WESLEY KITMACHER

Haunted
America

Published by Haunted America
A Division of The History Press
Charleston, SC
www.historypress.com

Front cover: The Columbia River, 2020. *Courtesy of Sonyuser, Pixabay.*
Back cover, top: An old steamboat, 1912. *Courtesy of WikiImages, Pixabay*;
bottom: The Columbia River, 2016. *Courtesy of 12019, Pixabay.*

First published 2022

Manufactured in the United States

ISBN 9781467150569

Library of Congress Control Number: 2022937929

Notice: The information in this book is true and complete to the best of our knowledge. It is offered without guarantee on the part of the author or The History Press. The author and The History Press disclaim all liability in connection with the use of this book.

I dedicate this book to my beloved family.

CONTENTS

Introduction

Why I Wrote This Book

As a resident of the Pacific Northwest—the Astoria, Oregon area to be exact—I'm fascinated by the area's history and culture. The Pacific Northwest was one of the last parts of the United States to be explored and settled, making it seem more "wild" than other parts of the country. In my book *Haunted Graveyard of the Pacific*, I focused on hauntings at the mouth of the Columbia River, where the river meets the Pacific Ocean, as well as the coastal areas between Portland, Oregon, and Seattle, Washington. Some believe the term "Graveyard of the Pacific" applies only to the confluence of the Pacific Ocean and the Columbia River. In fact, the Graveyard stretches along the Pacific Northwest coast, from Tillamook Bay in Oregon, past the treacherous Columbia Bar (the world's most dangerous entrance to a commercial waterway) near Astoria, Oregon, up the Washington coast, the Juan de Fuca strait separating Canada from the United States and up the western coast of Vancouver Island. Further, the Graveyard includes the waterways and the coasts that hug those waters.

The Columbia River has gone by many names in Native languages as well as English and Spanish: Nch'i-Wana (the Great River), the Big River, the River of the West, the Thegayo, the Rio de los Reyes, the Rio Estrachos and the Rio de Aguilar. This mighty river, the second largest after the Mississippi by volume in the United States, unites all parts of the Pacific Northwest.

The Columbia River, 2020. *Courtesy of Sonyuser, Pixabay.*

Historically, the river garnered much interest on the part of explorers of many nations, including Spain, Great Britain and the United States. These countries struggled over possession of the river as they sought the legendary Northwest Passage. Their hope, unfulfilled, was to find a direct route by water from the Mississippi River to the Pacific Ocean. This is what led to President Thomas Jefferson commissioning the Lewis and Clark Expedition. This competition between nations, as well as the settling of the region, led to much pathos, tragedy, opportunity and achievement.

There is no better way to discover the beauty and history of the Pacific Northwest than to explore the Pacific coast, the Columbia River, the Snake River and the towns near their shores. In this book, I examine reported hauntings, folkloric tales and supernatural creatures said to inhabit the areas along and near the Columbia and Snake Rivers, tributaries from Oregon and Washington to the Idaho border and nearby coastal areas. While the Pacific Northwest offers breathtaking scenery, it has also been identified as one of the most haunted regions in the United States. The spirits of the frontiersmen, adventurers, boatmen and early settlers seem to cling to the rivers, lakes, shores and towns.

At the western end of the Columbia River lies Astoria, Oregon, a rustic, beautiful Victorian coastal city established in 1811. It is the oldest permanent

American settlement west of the Rocky Mountains and is often referred to as the "San Francisco of the Northwest" due to its hilly topography and distinct architecture. To the east of Astoria, through Oregon, Washington and to the Idaho border, are rustic villages, restaurants, antique stores, surf shops and carnivals, while farmers' markets and weekly tourist festivals welcome residents and visitors alike. The Pacific Northwest is known for great hiking, boating, camping, fishing, biking, clamming, golfing, cranberry cultivation, oyster farming and tourism, while state parks with nineteenth-century military forts and national historic sites welcome history enthusiasts. Bald eagles, black bears, elk, deer and other wildlife call the area home.

Despite this idyllic setting, more than two thousand ships and countless lives have been lost to the treacherous waters where the Pacific Ocean meets the Columbia River, to the north and south and east along the rivers and tributaries. Smaller rivers in Oregon and Washington feed the mighty Columbia River as it races toward the Pacific Ocean. The combination of river flow and offshore currents creates an ever-shifting, hazardous sandbar at the mouth of the 1,214-mile-long Columbia River. Unlike other rivers whose power dissipates as they drain into deltas, the Columbia River funnels water like a powerful firehose into the Pacific Ocean. This, together with frequent thick fog, violent storms and man-made disasters, has caused ships to sink, burn and be crushed against the shore.

On land, the spirits of settlers and adventurers are said to linger in places like Astoria and Portland, Oregon, and along the shores of the Columbia and Snake Rivers. In the nineteenth century, the Oregon Trail, which stretched from Missouri to the Pacific Ocean and hugged the Columbia River, served as a major route for those wishing to travel west to discover new land and begin new lives. But the Oregon Trail was dangerous, and as many as thirty-four thousand lives were lost along the trail to disease, accidents and more. Other lingering spirits are said to include those of Native Americans whose lands were stolen and burial grounds desecrated, soldiers, murderers and murder victims.

In addition to shipwrecks, drownings and shanghaiing, there are other reasons supernatural tales and folklore abound in the Pacific Northwest. The geography and climate of the Pacific Northwest—towering trees, mountains, volcanoes, icy waters, earthquakes, tsunamis, high winds—are part of a long record of natural events that were not easy for Native Americans and others to make sense of without some supernatural explanation. Native Americans have long-standing beliefs in Sasquatch, sea monsters, Thunderbirds, werewolves and other creatures that help explain

Painting of a ship, 2015. *Courtesy of Comfreak, Pixabay.*

A forest in fog, 2016. *Courtesy of LUM3N, Pixabay.*

the unexplainable. The wildness of the region, as the last portion of the continental United States to be settled, influences such supernatural tales. There is also a strong Scandinavian influence in the Pacific Northwest, bringing with it an abundance of supernatural folklore and tales.

Chilling tales of paranormal phenomena abound in this northwestern corner of America, and it's no wonder movies and television shows like the vampire and werewolf book and movie series *Twilight* saga, the pirate treasure movie *The Goonies*, the TV series *Supernatural*, the remake of *The Fog* and the drama-mystery *Twin Peaks* were made or based in the Pacific Northwest. Even the movie *The Shining*, for which Oregon's Timberline Lodge served as the movie's Colorado-based Stanley Hotel for exterior shots, featured a package of "Willapoint Minced Clams," sourced in the Graveyard of the Pacific, at Willapa Bay, Washington.

The dark skies, wind and fog that frequent the Pacific Northwest round out the atmosphere of mystery and dread. So, if you see someone on land who appears out of place or hear ghostly words on the wind, check again—it might be the forlorn spirit of a lost soul reaching out.

My Beliefs and Approach

Those who believe in ghosts, supernatural creatures and paranormal phenomena say restless spirits haunt the Pacific Northwest, while others point to the tales of Native Americans and early settlers. Though I would not describe myself as a full believer in these stories, I find them fascinating and would like to believe that some, or at least part, of the legends are true.

My background is an eclectic one that, while on the surface might not appear to tie directly to the subjects I write about, prepared me for this work. I retired from the U.S. government in 2019 after thirty-six years as a senior executive, manager and in other roles in the western United States and Washington, D.C. I am also a consultant, legal expert witness and licensed attorney. From the early 1980s to the mid-2000s, while based in the San Francisco Bay area, I made numerous trips throughout the Pacific Northwest to teach government leadership courses. It was during that time that I became fascinated by the region's atmosphere and history.

My wife, Wendy, and I moved from the West to Washington, D.C., for my work. My last role was that of chief human capital officer for a federal agency. I was named that agency's senior executive of the year for 2019. After living in the D.C. area for thirteen years, we retired and decided to move back west. Our focus quickly centered on the Pacific Northwest. Part of our reasoning was economic (no income tax in Washington and no sales tax in Oregon!), but much of our decision-making focused on the climate, history and beauty of the area. Upon retiring, I quickly found I had no desire to *fully* retire; I had to do something more, something worthwhile that would reflect my desire to acclimate to my new home and have a positive impact. To paraphrase American stateman Benjamin Franklin, if one wishes to be remembered, they should either write something worth reading or do something worth writing about. I chose the former!

I have also served as a college professor at Georgetown University in Washington, D.C.; Portland State University in Oregon; Grays Harbor College in Aberdeen, Washington; and Clatsop Community College in Astoria, Oregon. In addition to *Haunted Graveyard of the Pacific* and this book, I wrote *Monsters and Miracles: Horror, Heroes, and the Holocaust*, a book that blends family stories with World War II and Holocaust history, as well as folklore, heroic tales and horror stories. *Monsters and Miracles* was published internationally by Amsterdam Publishers, the leading publisher of Holocaust memoirs in Europe, in the summer of 2022.

I have also developed a course on the haunted history and folklore of the Pacific Northwest that I am teaching at Clatsop Community College. I have been featured in newspapers, on radio programs, at museums and in bookstores, where I have spoken about the haunted folklore of the Pacific Northwest. In the spring of 2022, I served as a speaker and instructor at the Oregon Ghost Conference in Seaside, Oregon. I designed and am leading haunted and history trolley tours of Washington State's Long Beach Peninsula. I am also a member of the Historical Writers' Association.

Using an evidence-based approach to research and analyze reported supernatural phenomena, I found a wealth of information on the region's haunted history in Native American oral history, settler and adventurer accounts and books, newspapers from the mid-1800s to present day, recorded stories, government records and social media. I have not included legends or stories that lack evidence, and I have taken great pains to include, in the bibliography, all of the source materials that I reviewed and that informed my writing, making sure to give credit where credit is due.

As an author, professor, attorney and former senior executive, it is my nature to question whether these tales are based on fact and logic. I pride myself on my careful research, which I have practiced over the last forty years while wearing many different professional hats. But in researching these tales, it is clear not everything can be proven beyond a reasonable doubt. As Thomas Edison said, "We don't know a millionth of one percent about anything."

Legends and tales of hauntings and supernatural creatures serve many purposes. For believers, these tales may simply document paranormal activity. For others, they may help to explain that which is not easily explained. For others still, much like the experience of telling ghost stories around a fire, such tales can be a fun escape from reality. Whatever the reason, these tales are a fascinating part of an area's history.

Folklore has a rich history. In many cases, tales were created by rural, frequently poor peasants and others, through which they expressed a shared identity by way of traditional stories. Folklore takes many forms, including material (art, architecture, textiles), music, narrative (legends, fairy tales) and verbal (jokes and proverbs). The term *folklore* was coined in 1846 by Englishman William Thoms, who used the phrase to replace the words "popular antiquities" and "popular literature." It differs from *history*, which is made up of past events and changes in society. It is thought that folklore gives us the wisdom to understand history from a different point of view. Folklore showcases humankind's problems and successes.

Haunted folklore has been part of human culture since the first century AD, when Roman author and statesman Pliny the Younger described the specter of an elderly man with a long beard and rattling chains who haunted a house in Athens, Greece. Other examples of haunted folklore include the ghost of Anne Boleyn, the second wife of British King Henry VIII, who was executed in 1536 for witchcraft, treason and other reasons; her spirit has been reported in the Tower of London where she was imprisoned and in her childhood home of Hever Castle. The ghost of Thomas Jefferson's vice president, Aaron Burr, who famously dueled and killed founding father Alexander Hamilton, has been reported roaming the streets of the West Village in New York City. Benjamin Franklin's ghost has been seen near the American Philosophical Society Library in Philadelphia, Pennsylvania. The Gettysburg, Pennsylvania battlefield where the July 1–3, 1863 Battle of Gettysburg took place (which many say changed the course of the American Civil War), has been the spot of numerous sightings of ghostly soldiers apparently still fighting the battle. The World War I battlefields of Gallipoli (Turkey) and the Somme (France) are also sites of numerous ghost sightings. British prime minister Winston Churchill reported seeing the spirit of America's sixteenth president, Abraham Lincoln, in 1944 at the White House. Churchill stepped out of the bath and reportedly said, "Good evening, Mr. President, you seem to have me at a disadvantage."

In my experience, some history purists bristle at the retelling of these folkloric tales. They dispute the topics and events as "not history" and therefore of little or no value. I disagree. Although folklore is not regarded as history by some, to many—including in the academic community—folklore is seen as an integral part of a region's history. Folklore is studied at Harvard, Berkeley and other leading universities and is considered an important way to understand different cultures. Further, folklore—especially haunted tales—draws the interest of people in a way that straight history too often does not. Folklore is defined as "the traditional beliefs, customs, and stories of a community, passed through the generations by word of mouth; a body of popular myth and beliefs related to a particular place." In this book, I intertwine folklore with history, and though I am clear about which is which, I believe the two go hand in hand.

I have written this book in the form of a road map, exploring the Pacific Northwest along the Columbia and Snake Rivers and through smaller tributaries and nearby land-based areas, intertwining long-standing tales, folklore and history. I view my role as multifaceted: historian, investigator, interested taleteller, prideful resident and tour guide. It is through these lenses

The Columbia River area, 2017. *Courtesy of chapay, Pixabay.*

that I wrote this book. As humans, we have particularly short memories; few remember tragedies that happened decades, let alone a century, ago. Other than the *Titanic* and a few notable others, we have virtually no memory of long-ago shipwrecks that resulted in multiple deaths. These disasters were all too common in the days before satellite navigation, GPS and cellphones. With this in mind, one of my primary reasons for writing books like this is to try to help preserve historical stories that might be lost over time.

Please join me as we journey along the breathtaking Columbia and Snake Rivers, tributaries and coastal areas. I hope you enjoy reading this book as much as I enjoyed writing it!

PART I

Haunted and Supernatural Sites Along the Columbia River, Other Waterways and Nearby

CHAPTER 1

GHOSTS AND OTHER UNDEAD

Of those surveyed for a 2017 *USA Today* article, 45 percent stated they believe in ghosts, 32 percent said they believe ghosts can hurt the living and 18 percent reported having been in the presence of a ghost. This belief in ghosts has existed for as long as humans have inhabited the Earth; it is not a new phenomenon. Tales of ghosts were present in ancient Egypt, Mesopotamia, ancient Greece, the Roman Empire, Native American and Aboriginal cultures and across many religions. To this day, haunted tales persist in many cultures and societies.

The scientific view is ghosts and supernatural phenomena are simply the products of optical illusions, hallucinations or other explainable maladies or logical errors.

For believers, ghosts and supernatural creatures can be good, evil or something in between. They may represent an omen or portent of death, or they may not. The word *ghost* comes from Old English and refers to the human spirit or soul of the deceased. It was thought that the spirit was separate from the deceased's physical body and could appear to the living. Ghosts or haunts are often thought of as spirits that have not passed on because they are trapped in this dimension, connected to earthly property, the living or some unfinished business to which they are trying to attend. Often, but not always, lingering spirits are said to be of the deceased who met sudden, unexpected and violent deaths. Another form of ghosts, graveyard spirits, are thought to haunt the locations where their physical bodies were buried after death. Though different cultures have different theories about ghosts, most have some belief in an afterlife.

Ghosts are said to generally take one of six forms:

- Ectoplasm or Ecto-Mist: a vaporous cloud floating above the ground that appears white, gray or black. Reportedly witnessed in graveyards, battlefields and historical sites, among other places.
- Funnels: experienced in homes or historical buildings as cold spots, wisps or swirling spirals of light. Many of us have experienced cold spots and wondered if it's an air circulation issue or perhaps something more sinister.
- Inanimate Objects: ghost ships, ghost trains and other vehicles believed to be controlled by the undead who died in accidents or wrecks or suffered sudden and unexpected ends. Examples include the old *City of Albany* ghost train featured in 1989's *Ghostbusters II* (really an amalgam of multiple train wrecks), said to have killed over one hundred people after it derailed in 1920; and the *Flying Dutchman*, a legendary ghost ship said to be doomed to sail forever, most likely based on seventeenth-century Dutch East India Company ships.
- Interactive Personality: the spirit of a known deceased person, family member or historical figure. The spirit is said to be able to make itself visible, speak or otherwise let someone know it is present. It may be visiting to comfort the living or perhaps because it believes the living want to see them. An example is when British prime minister Churchill reported seeing the spirit of President Lincoln.
- Orbs: a transparent or translucent hovering ball of light. Sometimes orbs go unnoticed but are captured in a photo or video. These entities are often seen in television ghost-hunter programs.
- Poltergeist: German for "noisy ghost," a poltergeist is thought to be able to move or knock things over, make noise, manipulate the physical environment, turn lights on and off, slam doors and start fires. They are often depicted as dangerous, as seen in the 1982 Steven Spielberg horror movie *Poltergeist*.

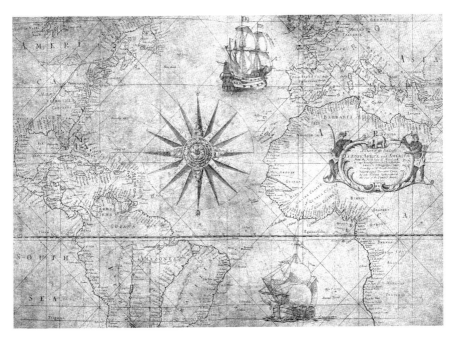

Image of a nautical map, 2020. *Courtesy of Darkmoon, Pixabay.*

As shown in books and movies, the undead are also thought to be able to take on forms other than ghosts and are often portrayed as evil, vengeful creatures that prey on the living. These supernatural beings are said to take on the forms of:

- Monsters: naturally occurring or man-made supernatural creatures
- Mummies: intentionally preserved corpses
- Vampires: undead creatures that feed on the blood of humans and other living beings
- Werewolves: people who transform into wolf-like creatures
- Zombies: reanimated corpses that feed on flesh

CHAPTER 2

SUPERNATURAL CREATURES

Cryptozoology is a pseudoscience that seeks to prove the existence of supernatural, folkloric creatures. Cryptozoologists refer to the creatures they seek to prove exist as *cryptids*, and such creatures include Bigfoot, the Loch Ness monster and the Thunderbird. According to a 2012 Angus Reid public opinion poll, nearly 29 percent of Americans and 21 percent of Canadians believe Bigfoot is "definitely" or "probably" real. It is also worth noting that some creatures that were once thought to exist only in folklore do really exist (the gorilla, giant squid and okapi, to name a few).

The supernatural creatures described in this book include:

- Sea Serpents: legendary snake, dragon and dinosaur-like creatures said to inhabit the ocean and rivers. Described in various cultures' mythology, including Native American, Greek, Norse, biblical and others.
- Bigfoot: also known as Sasquatch, Omah, Yowie, Yeti and the Abominable Snowman, Bigfoot is portrayed as a large, ape-like creature with huge feet that stands between seven and ten feet tall. Bigfoot is said to inhabit North American forests, and folklore can be found in Native American culture, in stories brought to the United States by Finnish and European settlers and in the tales of loggers, miners, trappers and prospectors.
- Thunderbirds: Native American legendary large bird-like creatures said to possess supernatural power and strength sufficient to cause thunder when they flap their wings.

CHAPTER 3
NAUTICAL SUPERSTITIONS

P aranormal activity along the Columbia River, Snake River and other tributaries is heavily influenced by nautical legends and superstitions. To paraphrase a nineteenth-century fatalistic belief among sailors, "What the waters want, the waters will have." As many sailors could not swim, even bathing in the ocean or rivers presented a dangerous challenge. Fear of the water gave rise to nautical superstitions, many of which remain to this day.

It is considered unlucky to begin a voyage on a Friday because Jesus was crucified on a Friday. Seeing a person with red hair or someone who was cross-eyed or flat-footed was thought to bring bad luck. As flowers, ministers and ringing bells were associated with funerals, seeing or hearing them before a voyage was thought to forecast death and bad luck; if someone's spouse brought flowers onto the ship, the flowers were thrown overboard. While the crew intentionally ringing the ship's bells was exempt from superstition, the bells ringing on their own—even if caused by the wind—was thought to portend death. Killing an albatross, gull or dolphin was thought to mean bad luck, as was stepping aboard with your left foot, losing a bucket overboard or seeing rats run off the ship. The presence of umbrellas onboard or clapping your hands on a ship was thought to tempt thunder and bad weather. Throwing stones into the water was thought to trigger storms and huge swells.

The old adage "Red sky in the morning, sailors take warning. Red sky at night, sailors' delight" is thought to have some basis in fact. When we see a red sky at night, meteorologists say the setting sun's light is passing through

Photo of a seagull, 2017. *Courtesy of JanBaby, Pixabay.*

dust particles, indicating high pressure, stable air and good weather to come. When we see a red sky in the morning, it is thought the high pressure and good weather have already passed and that low pressure or a storm might be on the way. Strange sounds heard at sea were often blamed on sirens or mermaids, who were believed to lure sailors to their deaths. As the sight of a bare-breasted woman was thought to calm angry waters, ships' figureheads were often carvings of bare-breasted, well-endowed women. Ending a ship's name with the letter "a" was also considered unlucky, and some believe the vessels *Lusitania* and *Britannia*, which were sunk by German torpedoes, illustrate this point.

Other long-standing nautical superstitions include the warning to never paint your ship green, as doing so will cause the vessel to beach itself in a gale. Turning a cup or bucket upside down was thought to cause a boat to capsize, and whistling in the wheelhouse was believed to provoke high winds. Once heading to a ship, one should never turn back, and saying the word *pig* was to be avoided at all costs. Many disasters are said to be linked to the violation of these superstitions.

PART II

HAUNTED AND
SUPERNATURAL RIVER
JOURNEY (WEST TO EAST)

Map of the Lewis and Clark Expedition, 2014. *Courtesy of Photoman, Pixabay.*

CHAPTER 1

ASTORIA, OREGON

"Most Wicked Place on Earth"

O ur first stop is Astoria, Oregon. Founded in 1811, the beautiful, rustic, riverfront city of Astoria is Oregon's oldest city and the site of America's first settlement west of the Rocky Mountains. Astoria is located on the southern coast of the Columbia River, where the river flows into the Pacific Ocean. Astoria is named after John Jacob Astor, an investor and entrepreneur from New York City. Astor's American Fur Company founded Fort Astoria and established a monopoly in the fur trade business in the early nineteenth century. Interestingly, John Jacob Astor never visited Oregon or this city named for him. Astoria was incorporated by the Oregon Legislative Assembly on October 20, 1876, but with its great number of wood structures, it burned down seven years later in 1883 and again in 1922. Both times, Astoria was rebuilt at a higher level, away from the waters of the Columbia River, resulting in tunnels under the city.

Astoria has remained the center of reported paranormal activity for well over a century. The 2007 horror movie *Cthulhu*, based on H.P. Lovecraft's 1936 book *Shadow over Innsmouth*, was filmed in Astoria and based on Astoria legends. Most recently, in 2018, the Travel Channel program *Ghost Adventures* produced a four-episode segment focusing on Astoria, the neighboring area and the Graveyard of the Pacific. Instead of Astoria, a better name for the city may be "Ghostoria," as many ghosts are thought to inhabit the area.

Astoria has a rich and colorful (blood red, some would say!) history. Although other towns may make the claim to fame, Astoria was once described by a journalist as the "most wicked place on earth." One of the

Photo of Astoria, Oregon fishing boats, 1941. *Courtesy of Russell Lee, Library of Congress.*

reasons for this description was a man named Bunko Kelly, an English hotelier and the leading shanghaier or crimper of the late nineteenth century, who is thought to have kidnapped thousands of sailors in Astoria, Portland and elsewhere to unwillingly serve onboard ships heading to Asia. Kelly is also said to have kidnapped women to serve as prostitutes and slaves. By his own account, Kelly said he shanghaied and kidnapped over two thousand men and women over a fifteen-year period from 1879 to 1894. He set a record for crimping by kidnapping and providing a ship's captain with fifty men over a three-hour period. One of Kelly's nicknames was the "King of the Crimps," and he was given the additional nickname of "Bunko" due to his providing a ship's captain with a wooden cigar store Indian in place of a human sailor. That was not the only time Bunko cheated a ship's captain, as in 1893, he shanghaied twenty-two men in Portland who had been drinking embalming fluid in a funeral home (apparently thinking it was alcohol) and provided the sailors to the captain of the *Flying Prince*, only to have the captain discover all of the sailors dead the next day. Bunko Kelly was never arrested for crimping, as it was inexplicably not illegal to shanghai someone at that time. Kelly was, however, arrested for murder in 1894, convicted in 1895 and sent to the Oregon State Penitentiary in Salem. He was released from prison in

1908. He subsequently wrote the book *Thirteen Years in the Oregon Penitentiary*, traveled to California and was never seen or heard from again.

The word *shanghaier* is thought to refer to the fact that the kidnappings occurred primarily in the Chinatown sections of towns or because many ships were headed to Shanghai and elsewhere in Asia. The word *crimping* is thought to refer either to the British term for impressing sailors to unwillingly serve aboard ships or to the Dutch word for live fish kept in a tank of water. Unsuspecting sailors were shanghaied from local bars, boardinghouses and even while walking down the sidewalk, taken through the underground tunnels and forced to serve on ships in need of crews. There are many haunted tales of disembodied voices, cold spots, unexplained noises and other phenomena that are based in Portland's, Astoria's and Seattle's undergrounds, said to be related to the ghosts of shanghaied sailors, kidnapped women and others who were transported through or worked in the tunnels.

In addition to the crimping, gambling houses, brothels, saloons, opium dens and worse were common in Astoria in the late 1800s. Thousands of shipwrecks that claimed countless lives occurred in the nearby hazardous, fog-enshrouded waters where the Columbia River meets the Pacific Ocean. Bodies of unidentified drowning victims washed ashore nearby. It is said Astoria's long-standing brutal history makes it prime territory for lingering spirits.

A lifesaving ring, 2016. *Courtesy of kla3950, Pixabay.*

The Norblad Hotel, described as "hip" and unique, is a thirty-three-room historic mansion in Astoria and was one of the locations visited by the Travel Channel's *Ghost Adventures* in 2018. The Norblad opened in January 1923, making it the oldest continuously operating hotel in Astoria. It is said to have a history of crime and violence. While there, the *Ghost Adventures* cast and crew visited the basement, where it is said there is an "unholy" presence. The hotel is said to house thousands of haunted objects, some so frightening and powerful they can't be touched, including Peggy the Doll, which causes heart attacks, and the infamous "Dybbuk Box," believed to be haunted by a malicious spirit.

The luxurious Officer's Inn Bed and Breakfast (B&B) in the Hammond neighborhood of nearby Warrenton, Oregon, is said to be haunted. It was originally built at the U.S. Army's nearby Fort Stevens base in 1905 as housing for army officers and their families and later became a B&B. The B&B's ghostly reputation attracted ghost hunting groups from Seattle and Portland. It is said some rooms are haunted. In one reported haunting, a couple stayed at the inn with their Labrador retriever. The next morning over breakfast, the woman shared an unusual experience she had during the night. She reported she was awakened in the middle of the night by her dog, which was cowering by her bedside. The dog jumped up in bed with her, its tail between its legs (behavior it had never before demonstrated). As the woman comforted the dog and looked around the room, the window shade began to flutter as if moved by ghostly hands. Other reported phenomena include unexplained cold spots, locked doors opening on their own, spirit-like figures glimpsed in empty rooms and rumpled bedspreads in unoccupied rooms where no one had slept.

Fort Stevens was one of three coastal defense forts (in addition to Forts Canby and Columbia in Washington State) built to protect the mouth of the Columbia River from possible foreign attack. It was an active base from 1863 to 1947 and has the distinction of being the only military installation in the contiguous United States to be attacked since the War of 1812. It is now an Oregon state park.

On June 21, 1942, the Japanese *I-25* submarine opened fire on Fort Stevens and seventeen shells landed on the fort, though they did not cause significant damage. Soldiers later remembered the attack causing confusion, resulting in a "real mad house." One U.S. soldier cut his head while rushing to his battle station. The ten-inch guns of the fort's Battery Russell were damaged by shells, as was the fort's baseball diamond and a power line. The *I-25*'s shells left craters on the beach and marshland around the fort.

Touring the fort's abandoned, historic structures has been described by some as unnerving. Guests and state park staff have described seeing the phantoms of soldiers—one in full battle gear, one carrying a long knife and another carrying a flashlight—wandering the fort's grounds, appearing to be in search of possible enemy soldiers. Two of the ghostly soldiers appear to be dressed in Civil War–era uniforms, while the other is dressed in World War II–era clothes. A man described walking around the grounds and seeing a soldier dressed in a World War II uniform. The man and the ghostly soldier nodded to each other as they passed, but when the man turned around, the soldier was gone.

Disembodied voices and footsteps, faint wailing, voices saying "get out," the feeling of someone watching visitors and glowing orbs have been reported at Fort Stevens. The stories of these ghosts are usually connected to unexplainable noises and rushes of cold air. It would appear that the dramatic submarine attack caused spirits to become tied to Fort Stevens, where they remain in defense of the battery and fort. The Travel Channel program *Ghost Adventures* visited the fort in 2018 to investigate the hauntings.

The historic Commodore Hotel, described as a premier boutique hotel, is also known for being one of the most haunted hotels in Oregon.

The Astoria-Megler Bridge, 2018. *Courtesy of Emil 02050, Pixabay.*

Panoramic photo of Astoria, Oregon, 1912. *Courtesy of Frank Woodfield, Library of Congress.*

It was built in 1925 to host passengers waiting to take ferryboats across the Columbia River to Washington. For unknown reasons, the hotel was boarded up in 1965 by its owner, who walked away from it. It was closed for forty years, renovated beginning in 2007 and reopened in 2009. One guest described the very small hallways of the hotel, in which photos of the hotel over the years are displayed, as enhancing a feeling of foreboding. Another guest commented on the "spookiness" of the hotel. The hotel has conducted "Dark Arts" events and separately has been visited by ghost investigators. Several spirits are reportedly present, including that of a child said to be "trapped at the hotel" and an Asian man who came to Astoria as a laborer in the 1800s, among others.

The Rogue Ales Public House is located in the former Bumble Bee Tuna's Hanthorn Cannery on Pier 39 in Astoria, overlooking the Columbia River. The cannery was active from 1875 to 1981. It is now a museum dedicated to the former salmon canning facility and is located on the pier that housed the former cannery that employed children as laborers. It has been reported that a little girl fell off the pier in the late 1800s or early 1900s and drowned. Staff and patrons of the pub have said they think she still haunts the pier where she died. Around the pub's closing time and often after hours, staff have reported seeing lights turning on and off on their own and have heard disembodied ghostly laughter.

The historic Hotel Elliott, filled with old-world charm, was opened by Chester Trabucco in 1924, two years after the town of Astoria was nearly leveled by the 1922 fire. It is in the heart of downtown Astoria, a few blocks from the waterfront. It is said that the spirit of a guest who stayed at the hotel

some eighty years ago still haunts the premises. The spirit makes its presence known with disembodied footsteps, cold spots, items found moved from their original locations and other strange disturbances.

The Rosebriar Inn, a beautiful mansion built in 1902, sits on a hill above downtown with wonderful views of the Columbia River. It's said the spirit of a visiting nun roams the halls. Though her spirit is thought to mean no harm, it is unclear why her spirit remains at the inn.

Based on its many hauntings, Astoria has certainly earned its nickname of "Ghostoria."

CHAPTER 2

SUPERNATURAL CREATURES

The Columbia River Sea Serpent, Bigfoot and Thunderbirds

SEA SERPENTS

When most residents are asked, the first Pacific Northwest creature that comes to mind is Sasquatch or Bigfoot. There have been numerous reported sightings of this creature over the last century and beyond. But Sasquatch is not the only reported legendary creature. The Columbia Bar sea serpent nicknamed "Colossal Claude" has been reported regularly as well.

Some people who believe sea serpents exist speculate that a group of plesiosaurus (extinct marine reptiles from the Mesozoic and Jurassic ages) survived and live in the Columbia River and other Pacific Northwest waterways. Scientists say these creatures ranged from 5.0 to 49.0 feet in length and were some of the largest apex predators on record, with a skull length of 7.3 to 9.4 feet. Scientists believe the plesiosaurus went extinct in the Cretaceous-Paleogene event that killed off the dinosaurs about sixty-six million years ago. Those who believe the theory say at least one of these creatures survived in the deeper parts of the Columbia River, feeding on the salmon that populate its waters.

The oral histories of Pacific Northwest Natives, including the Kwakwaka, Tlingit and Haidas tribes, describe fantastic sea creatures with names such as *sisiutl* and *wasgo*. The legends are based along the coasts of Vancouver Island, British Columbia and southeast Alaska, and these creatures are described as large and snakelike. The first non-Native sightings of sea serpents were reported in newspapers and publications, including the *Sunday Oregonian*'s 1905 "Caught by a Savage Sea Toad," the *Oregon Sunday Journal*'s 1906 "Sea Serpents Are Not Summer Resort Delusions," the *Oregonian*'s 1911 "The Great White Serpent of the Malorili: A Tale of Love and Adventure" and the *Oregonian*'s 1913 "Sea Serpents: They Are a Reality and Not a Myth."

Another early non-Native report of a Columbia River sea serpent occurred in March 1934. The lightship tender (known by this designation under the

A dinosaur skull, 2015. *Courtesy of Viergacht, Pixabay.*

former U.S. Lighthouse Service, which was merged in 1939 into the U.S. Coast Guard, now known as a buoy tender under the current Coast Guard; this vessel services lighthouses and tends buoys, hauls supplies and conducts search-and-rescue and law enforcement operations) *Rose* had just returned from dropping off a relief crew on the Columbia River Lightship (a vessel that acted as a lighthouse, which is now mostly obsolete—replaced with lighthouses and large automated buoys). The *Rose* and lightship crews reported seeing a huge, snakelike creature swimming around the ships. L.A. Larson, first mate on the *Rose*, reported that it was forty feet long with an eight-foot-long neck, a "mean-looking" tail and a snakelike head. Captain J. Jensen of the *Rose* told the *Morning Oregonian* newspaper that the snakelike creature's head looked more like a camel than a snake but agreed on most other details.

The *Rose*'s crew, after watching the strange creature with binoculars for a short period of time, asked the captain if they could launch a small boat and approach it for a better view. The ship's officers, afraid the creature was big enough to tip the boat, ordered the men not to. Eventually, the serpent slipped away, out of sight. The creature was nicknamed "Colossal Claude."

After three months, a strange carcass was reported washed ashore on southwest Washington State's Long Beach Peninsula. Some speculated it could be the sea serpent, but others said it was most likely an oarfish or decomposed whale shark. After minimal reporting, the story faded from discussion.

A few years later, in 1937, the sea serpent was again in the news. The crew of the fishing trawler *Viv* reported they observed Claude and that the serpent

A Native canoe, 2016. *Courtesy of Mrs. Brown, Pixabay.*

had spent time studying them up close. Captain Charles Graham of the *Viv* described it as a tan, hairy, forty-foot-long creature with a horselike head.

A few months after the *Viv* sighting in 1937, the Whites, a couple visiting the Devil's Churn, a narrow inlet of the Pacific Ocean 120 miles to the south, reported sighting the creature. The Whites were visiting when they saw, just offshore, what they described as a fifty-five-foot-long, hairy, giraffelike creature whose head and neck were sticking fifteen feet out of the water. The creature headed south along the coast, and the Whites, hoping to catch a second glimpse, ran to their car and raced after it as it made for Heceta Head (a one-thousand-foot-tall headland above the Pacific Ocean). There, they again sighted the sea serpent before it turned and headed out to sea.

On April 13, 1939, the crew of the fishing boat *Argo* reported the closest sighting yet of the creature as it made its way through the Columbia River. Captain Chris Anderson reported the creature passed within ten feet of the *Argo*, its head and neck rising ten feet above the waves. Anderson said one of his crew members used a boat hook to try to poke the creature but that Anderson stopped him out of fear of agitating the creature and it sinking the boat. The captain observed that the creature had a camel-like head with coarse gray fur and glassy eyes. The *Argo*'s was the last confirmed sighting of the Columbia Bar sea serpent until decades later.

The next recorded sighting of Colossal Claude occurred in 1989. That year, a fishing crew was dragging a net when it snagged on something in the water. The snag started to pull the bow of the ship downward into the water. Captain Donald Riswick was finally able to pull the net in and found a hole had been torn. The net was several hundred feet long, had been snagged at about thirty feet deep and had a tear in it that was several feet across. These incidents were attributed, by those speculating on this theory, to a giant serpent.

Riswick's spotting was the end of the reported sightings in the northwest Oregon and southwest Washington portions of the Columbia River. Rumor has it the creature moved on to other parts of the Columbia River or the Pacific Ocean. Others have speculated that Colossal Claude is some sort of large jellyfish, while others continue to argue that it is left over from the prehistoric era. No one knows what type of cryptid Colossal Claude is. Like the Yeti, Bigfoot or Loch Ness monster, science has yet to prove or disprove Colossal Claude's existence.

The North Coast's second legendary celebrity is Marvin, who was originally spotted in 1963. That year, Shell Oil Company divers searching for oil observed the fifteen-foot animal and recorded the encounter on tape. Some believe Marvin and Claude are the same creature. During a viewing of the recording, observers gave the creature the nickname "Marvin the Monster." Adding to the description of Claude, they indicated the creature had barnacled bumps and ridges and swam in a spiral motion in over 180 feet of water. Some of America's leading marine biologists have studied the recording and debated how to explain what was observed.

It is worth noting that another sea serpent has reportedly been spotted in the Pacific Northwest. It is known as the Ogopogo and has been seen swimming in the sixty-mile-long Lake Chelan in north central Washington, a lake surrounded by the jagged Cascade Mountains. It is described as a creature with a long, powerful tail. Reports of sightings date back more than 150 years. Some say either the same or a similar creature has been observed swimming in Lake Okanagan, British Columbia.

Although sightings of sea serpents have been scarce over the past several decades, Claude, Marvin and the Ogopogo are testaments to the supernatural sightings that are relatively common in the Pacific Northwest. Astoria's Columbia River Maritime Museum, which "launched" my first book, *Haunted Graveyard of the Pacific*, on July 25, 2021, has even held a Sea Monster Day.

BIGFOOT

Bigfoot (also known as Sasquatch, Omah, Yowie, Yeti and the Abominable Snowman) has been reported throughout Oregon and Washington State, including along the Columbia River. The creature is said to be a large apelike creature that inhabits the forests of North America. Some believe Bigfoot is in fact a Gigantopithecus, a gigantic ape that stood ten feet tall, weighed up to 1,200 pounds and lived beside early humans for over one million years. Fortunately for man, this enormous ape's diet was almost exclusively bamboo. However, scientists believe the Gigantopithecus went extinct 100,000 years ago in the Pleistocene period. Those who believe Bigfoot exists dispute scientists' findings.

Whether real or not, Bigfoot has been the subject of countless books, movies and advertising campaigns. Skamania County in Washington State, located to the east of Vancouver, Washington, passed a law in 1969 regarding Bigfoot, declaring, "Any willful, wanton slaying of such creatures shall be deemed a felony subject to a substantial fine and/or imprisonment."

The county commissioner insisted the new law was not a joke. Sightings have been so plentiful and frequent that in 1970, a man named Peter Byrne established the Bigfoot Research Project (BRP) in Mount Hood, Oregon, along the Columbia River, which serves as a central clearing house of information on the mysterious humanoid.

Legends of Sasquatch and Bigfoot abound in the Pacific Northwest. Some people swear they've seen and heard these large apelike creatures. The origin of the Bigfoot legends may be tied to both Native and, separately, European folklore surrounding the "wild man." Natives strongly believed the Sasquatch was real. There are ancient tales of "wild men" who lurked near villages and left immense footprints. Members of the Plateau tribes, such as those at the Warm Springs Reservation in north-central Oregon, described Sasquatch as a "stick Indian," a potentially hostile being who stole salmon and confused people by whistling, causing them to become lost. The Pacific Northwest also has a large population of people whose ancestors traveled here from Finland, Norway and other Scandinavian countries. For centuries, there have been legends of "hairy wild men" in those countries.

As documented in 1865 by ethnographer George Gibbs, Pacific Northwest Natives described the creature Tsiatko as hirsute (covered with coarse, stiff hair) "wild Indians" of the woods. Natives told tales of these large, wild, hairy men. In 1898, Chief Mischelle of the Nlaka'pamux in British Columbia told the story of a creature he called "the benign-faced one." Members of

An Oregon Bigfoot statue, *Image of a Bigfoot*, 2018. *Courtesy of Carol M. Highsmith, Library of Congress.*

the Lummi tell tales of *Ts'emekwes*, while other tribes use different names, including *stiyaha*, *kwi-kwiyai* and *skoocooms*. Though most tales describe benign giants living among the people and stealing salmon from fishing nets, others describe dangerous and even cannibalistic creatures. According to a nineteenth-century legend, children were warned against saying the names of these creatures for fear that the beings would hear them and carry off or kill someone. To this day, tales of these beings are still told on reservations.

The Pacific Northwest is home to a significant number of proud Americans of Finnish descent, and their stories may have contributed to the Sasquatch legend. One Finnish mythical creature said to be found in the woods is the Peikko. The Peikko is reported to be a slow, large, hairy, apelike creature. Some are said to be aggressive, and they are thought to be related to trolls, giants and goblins. It could be that the legend of the Peikko, brought to America by immigrating Finns, added to Sasquatch sightings in the Pacific Northwest.

Sasquatch (or Bigfoot) began capturing the public's attention when it was first widely described in Oregon in 1904. Sightings of these hairy wild men were reported by settlers in the Coastal Range, with similar accounts spread by miners and hunters in later decades. In 1924, miners on Mount St. Helens claimed to have been attacked by giant "apes" in an incident that was widely reported in Oregon newspapers.

Around 1958, loggers to the east and west of the Cascade Mountains began reporting sightings of Sasquatch-like creatures and discovering their immense tracks along logging roads. Witnesses observed these beings crossing roads at night, striding furtively through forest and mountain terrain and digging for and eating ground squirrels.

In October 1970, a fifteen-year-old eyewitness described hunting with his father south of the Hood River near Highway 30. He said he saw a large, very fast and powerful apelike creature running by. He stated he wasn't frightened but rather thought the creature looked intelligent, running quietly with purpose, grace and power.

Another eyewitness in December 1975 reported spotting Bigfoot in the Cascade Locks area along Interstate 84, along the Columbia River in Hood River County, Oregon. The individual was driving home from Portland to Yakima, Washington, in the dark and rain with his wife, father and mother. He described seeing a large six- to seven-foot-tall creature with dark, wet fur running with arms swinging. At first, the witness thought it was a tall person wearing a fur coat and hood. The creature crossed in front of the witness's car, and the passengers could feel the car hit the creature's leg. They described how the creature made eye contact with the people in the car. The witness said he looked straight into the creature's face, which he described as having "total fright and terror in its eyes." He reported the incident to the State Patrol, who said they had received a number of similar reports about a creature that night, with several police officers reporting incidents.

In 1993, a middle-aged dentist and his wife were passengers aboard a train near The Dalles along the Columbia River. They described how at about 2:00 p.m., while the train made an unscheduled stop in the snow, they saw a dark, apelike creature step into a clearing at the edge of the river. They said the creature "hunkered down," as if looking at the train. The creature reportedly had hair on its legs that stuck out from the snow like "bell bottom pants." The couple was convinced they had seen a Sasquatch. An investigator for the Bigfoot Research Project observed that particular area of The Dalles had been the sight of repeated Bigfoot sightings over the years.

Thunderbirds

In 2005, scientists from the Oregon Archaeological Society excavated bones of ancient birds called Teratorn. These creatures had a wingspan of more than twenty-four feet, weighed more than 170 pounds and were most likely carnivores. It is thought these birds went extinct about twelve thousand years ago, as the last ice age ended. Some believe Thunderbirds are in fact Teratorn that somehow survived.

Virtually every Native American culture has legends of a giant, powerful, supernatural and magical bird, referred to as the Thunderbird. Many of these legends are found in the art, songs and oral histories of Pacific Northwest coastal cultures. The Thunderbird is said to be a close relative of the phoenix, the ancient Egyptian and Greek bird associated with the worship of the sun. The name *Thunderbird* is said to be based on the birds' wings making a thunderclap-like sound when in flight. Each Thunderbird's wing has been described as larger than a Native canoe and each feather the size of a canoe paddle. The Thunderbird's eyes were said to be glowing red in color, and lightning shot out of its talons. It was said the Thunderbird created storms when it flew, and at least two Thunderbirds were said to fly in the Pacific Northwest: the first in the Cascade Mountain range and the second in the Olympic Mountains of the Puget Sound.

The story continues that the first Thunderbird lived part of the time inside Mount St. Helens, with earthquakes and volcanic eruptions occurring when the huge creature rolled over in its sleep. The rest of the time, it lived along Spirit Lake, at the foot of Mount St. Helens. Natives said that when the Thunderbird was angry, the water bubbled and frothed. One Native legend has it that the Thunderbird attacked many other creatures until the raven killed it. After this, the Thunderbird's body fell into the Columbia River and formed several islands. Other theorists believe the Thunderbird is still alive and responsible for recent eruptions, including a catastrophic one in 1980. Natives were afraid of Spirit Lake and kept their distance because of the Thunderbird and other spirit beings said to inhabit the area.

A Native Thunderbird totem pole, 2014. *Courtesy of LonaE, Pixabay.*

Artist Paul Kane traveled to Mount St. Helens when it erupted in the 1840s, sketching and painting pictures of it. After returning a few days later and seeing the paintings of the volcano that Kane had painted, the Natives, who had strong beliefs in and fears of ghostly spirits, thought he must be a ghost and ran away.

The second Thunderbird was said to be friendlier toward people. Native lore has it that many generations ago, the Olympic Peninsula's Quileute people were starving because a giant killer whale ate all the fish they relied on. Their chieftain appealed for help to the Great Spirit, who summoned the mighty Thunderbird. The Thunderbird caught the killer whale in its claws and flew to the people, giving it to them to eat. The Thunderbird then flew to its home at the almost eight-thousand-foot-tall Mount Olympus. Although this Thunderbird was friendlier to people, it also valued its privacy. Hunters climbing Mount Olympus were scared away by ice and rocks that fell when the Thunderbird smelled them and caused there to be avalanches.

Supernatural explanations are often given for events that are not easily explained. This may be true for the Thunderbird as well, helping to explain natural phenomena like earthquakes and volcanic eruptions. Some experts believe the Natives may have mistaken large eagles, common in the area,

Drawing of a condor, 2021. *Courtesy of Vizetelly, Pixabay.*

with the legendary Thunderbird. Others believe the largest living bird in North America, the California condor, may have been mistaken for the Thunderbird.

The Lewis and Clark Expedition reported an interaction with a possible Thunderbird. On November 18, 1805, Captain Clark and a party of eleven visited Cape Disappointment, located in modern-day Pacific County, Washington. It was there that they saw the Pacific Ocean for the first time. One of the men killed a bird with a huge wingspan of over nine feet. Their description corresponds with that of a California condor. It is thought there was a small population of these birds in the Pacific Northwest mountains until they were hunted to extinction.

In the late 1960s and early 1970s, a number of southeast Washington State residents reported seeing a large bird with a wingspan similar to a small private airplane. In 2002, people living in the Togiak and Manokotak villages in Alaska reported seeing a bird much bigger than anything they had ever seen before. Also in 2002, an airplane pilot, carrying passengers to the Manokotak village, said he saw a giant bird with a wingspan of about fourteen feet, the size of a Cessna 207 aircraft, flying next to his aircraft. Interestingly, most of these reported sightings occurred near large stormfronts. Cryptozoologist have said that birds of this size would need the high winds common to a stormfront to be able to get off the ground.

Few other sections of the country can boast of the strange and mystical creatures and legends that abound in the Pacific Northwest. They accentuate and add to the supernatural and paranormal atmosphere.

CHAPTER 3
THE COLUMBIA

A "River of Floaters"

It seems that nearly every week, a body is found in the Columbia River and other nearby bodies of water. Fishermen have reeled in more than fish; they have hooked bodies floating in the rivers. Part of this is due to the area's love of the outdoors, easy access to rivers and abundance of bridges. Other contributing factors include homelessness, mental illness and suicide.

One fisherman compared it to reeling in something that looked like the "Creature from the Black Lagoon." The dead body wore cut-off jean shorts and a wedding ring. The fingers were spread out stiffly, and barnacles lined his back. Unfortunately, this creepy discovery wasn't unusual; it was part of the "summer of floaters" that occurred in the Portland area.

From July 2016 to July 2017, forty-five human corpses, or "floaters," were seen bobbing and drifting and were fished or pulled from Portland's Columbia and Willamette Rivers. Law enforcement has indicated an average of thirty-six bodies were discovered in the two rivers over the last several years. This number is greater than the number killed in Portland car crashes (twenty-three in 2019) and number of murders (thirty-five in 2019) in the area.

The greatest number of bodies are found in the summer, when warmer water causes decomposing corpses to fill with gas, bloat, become buoyant and surface. The number of drownings in Portland's rivers far exceeds those in comparable cities. River debris sometimes cuts up the floating bodies. The cold temperatures of area rivers help preserve the corpses, allowing law enforcement to better determine cause of death.

A Portland, Oregon bridge on the Columbia River, 2017. *Courtesy of parkluck, Pixabay.*

No doubt water temperature, strong currents and recreation contribute to the number of bodies discovered. Alcohol is another contributing factor. Portland is home to some who describe themselves as "hobo pirates"—homeless people who live on boats—and their bodies may account for some of those discovered.

Portland's river of floaters may contribute to another phenomenon that has occurred along the Pacific coast between northern Washington and southern British Columbia. Severed feet keep washing ashore along these coasts. These severed feet are found still in sneakers, hiking boots and other shoes. Some of the shoe brands found include three New Balance, two Nike and an Ozark Trail.

Since 2007, sixteen of these detached human feet have been found in Washington and British Columbia. Most of them are right feet. At least one discovered foot was analyzed by the British Columbia Coroners Service. They couldn't tell how long the foot had been in the water, but the regional coroner said the model of shoe had gone on the market after March 2013. The coroner is working with local police to see if any reported disappearances are connected to the discovery.

In 2007, the first two feet—both right feet—were found in British Columbia just six days apart. The Royal Canadian Mounted Police said that finding them in such a short timeframe was suspicious. In 2008, another five feet were found, including in Washington. Speculation about the origins of the feet has ranged from natural disasters, including a 2004 tsunami, to drug dealers, serial killers and human traffickers. Another theory is that at least some of the feet came from a 2005 plane crash off Quadra Island. Five men were onboard, but only one of the bodies was found. Others posit that the coast is being used as a dumping ground for victims of organized crime.

According to scientists who analyzed the feet, they were likely detached from bodies due to the push and pull of turbulent waves. Further, several of the feet have been identified as belonging to individuals who suffered from depression, other forms of mental illness and/or had been reported missing. The King County Medical Examiner's Office in Washington indicated that these individuals might have died by jumping off local bridges into the water; this could explain why there have been many corpses found floating around these waters. Detached feet were found most recently in 2019 along the Pacific Northwest coast

There are no absolute answers, and the mystery continues. One thing is clear—these events truly make the area a "graveyard" of the Pacific.

CHAPTER 4

DEATH ALONG THE OREGON TRAIL

The nineteenth-century Oregon Trail stretched approximately two thousand miles west from Missouri toward the Rocky Mountains and ended in Oregon's Willamette Valley. It was a major land route for those wishing to travel west, hugging the shores of the Columbia River part of the way. Awaiting these travelers was inexpensive, fertile land. However, the trail was dangerous; as many as thirty-four thousand lives were lost, one in ten migrants.

To be properly outfitted with equipment, supplies and clothes in the mid-1840s, settlers who traveled the Oregon Trail spent roughly $800 to $1,200 (about $28,000 in 2021). Many pioneers raised capital by selling farms and other possessions. Along the trail, they found high prices and scarce supplies, often requiring them to work in exchange for goods. One pioneer in 1864, Julius Merrill, described settlers having nothing but bacon, crackers, milk and water for dinner. He said they came across a ranch that was selling beef, potatoes and squash at the exorbitant prices of "beef, 25 cents per lb., potatoes, 50 cents per lb., squashes, 2 dollars each." He said the rancher intended to swindle and starve the settlers, who refused to buy the items.

Tremendous hardship and death were a too frequent occurrence for travelers along the Oregon Trail. It is estimated that one grave was dug every hundred miles to bury the trail's dead. The majority of deaths occurred due to diseases caused by poor sanitation, such as cholera and typhoid fever. Another major cause of death for adults and children was falling off wagons and getting run over. Many pioneers purchased firearms for protection, the first weapons they had owned, and mishaps occurred, causing injury and death. Other deaths on the trail were due to drowning in rivers, suicide, weather, stampeding livestock, fellow migrant attacks, lightning and gunpowder explosions. Migrants became accustomed to death, suffering each loss together, quickly burying their dead and pressing on in hopes of a better life. The following migrants' quotes are taken from the U.S. Bureau of Land Management (BLM)'s "History Bits and Westward Quotes":

> *Word was passed that a woman had been accidentally run over and killed instantly....The woman was getting down from the moving vehicle, her clothing caught on the break-rod, and she was thrown forward beneath the wheel.*
> —*Ellen James Bailey Lamborn, September 3, 1864*

> *Passed six fresh graves!...Oh, 'tis a hard thing to die far from friends and home—to be buried in a hastily dug grave without shroud or coffin—the clods filled in and then deserted, perhaps to be food for wolves.*
> —*Esther McMillan Hanna, 1852*

> *The great cause of diarrhea, which has proven to be so fatal on the road, has been occasioned in most instances by drinking water from holes dug in the riverbank and long marshes. Emigrants should be very careful about this.*
> —*Abigail Scott, June 8, 1852*

Native Americans generally tolerated wagon trains passing through their territories and even traded with migrants passing through. There were some conflicts between Natives and migrants along the trail, but they were relatively rare. It is estimated that between 1840 and 1860, Natives killed 362 migrants, and migrants killed 426 Natives.

As might be expected based on the suffering and deaths along the trail, ghost stories and reported sightings are plentiful. Some of these are based near an old logging camp called Rhododendron Village along the Columbia River Gorge near Mount Hood. Specifically, Laurel Hill on the Barlow Road (named for Oregon Trail pioneer Sam Barlow) was a terrifying descent for migrants. Wagons had to be lowered with block and tackle, with some ropes tearing, sending wagons hurtling down the hill to a deadly outcome. The alternative of traveling down rapids of the wild Columbia River was no better. This atmosphere of fear and death has spawned sightings of strange glowing orbs, appearing in photographs

Old tombstones, 2018. *Courtesy of Paul Henri, Pixabay.*

taken of old bunkhouses. These buildings are said to shake mysteriously when walked on and through. In one case, an old piano with a mirror on the front was photographed, and a woman's face, unseen in person, appeared in the mirror, as if she was sitting at the piano and playing. A door on the old mess hall where the cook slept is said to open by itself every morning at 4:00 a.m. In 2001, volunteer restoration staff discovered a pair of rock-covered graves, one for a pioneer and the other for a Native American. They took photos, and when the film was developed, strange glowing orbs could be seen hovering above the graves.

The Oregon Trail was key to the settling of the West, but at a terrible toll. The suffering and death experienced add to the sense of supernatural and paranormal foreboding that exists in the area.

CHAPTER 5
LONGVIEW, WASHINGTON

A Mansion and Mount Coffin

After departing coastal Oregon, our next stop is Longview, Washington. Longview was the location of the ominously named Mount Coffin, a Native American burial ground. The first white residents were Harry and Rebecca Jane Huntington in 1849. The area was initially named Monticello in honor of Thomas Jefferson's Virginia home, and it remained sparsely populated until 1918, when Missouri timber baron Robert Long moved his operation here. Longview was incorporated in February 1924 and continues to be a hardworking center of timber and cargo activity.

The Rutherglen Mansion, built in the 1920s by town founder and Long-Bell Lumber Company general manager J.D. Tennant, sits on top of a hill overlooking the Longview industrial area. Its stark white walls appear ghostly, especially outlined against the night's black sky and shrouds of trees. It's reported that the mansion served as a school for troubled teenage girls in the 1970s, and the director used to have the young women go outside and scream to release pent-up energy. One story includes mysterious disembodied screams heard echoing from the building. In another, the spirits of a couple murdered on their wedding night by a jealous ex-boyfriend are said to linger.

In another story, a woman was tidying up the beds in one room. She turned away, and when she turned back, she saw an indentation in the bed, as if someone or something had been lying on it. There have also been reports about a room in which visitors would wake in the middle of the night and see a figure reading while sitting on the windowsill.

Photo of hills, 2019. *Courtesy of 14006163, Pixabay.*

A Portland-based paranormal research team, hearing rumors of hauntings, visited the mansion and co-located 1920s restaurant and bed-and-breakfast built by J.D. Tennant. The paranormal team members explored the chapel in the mansion's top floor, used for weddings. One of the investigators recorded for any sounds and later reported capturing unexplained voices saying, "we like it" or "they like it."

Mount Coffin was once a 240-foot-high hill along the Columbia River near present-day Longview. Lieutenant William Robert Broughton, commander of the Royal Navy survey ship HMS *Chatham*, gave the basalt mound its name in October 1792. The Lewis and Clark Expedition, passing by the area in November 1805, called it a "remarkable knob." It no longer exists, as it was quarried and leveled in the 1940s, and its former location is now part of the flatland located at the Port of Longview and the Weyerhaeuser Mill. Mount Coffin may be aptly named given the reported paranormal activities said to occur there. It was given this name because it served as Native burial grounds for the Skillute, a Chinook-speaking tribe who practiced aboveground interment of their deceased. In 1835, American naturalist John Kirk Townsend explored Mount Coffin and described the Native burial site as consisting of many canoes (many Pacific Northwest Native tribes buried their dead in canoes) containing Native bodies carefully wrapped in animal skins and blankets and supplied with fishing spears, weapons and other personal effects.

The belief in haunted Native burial grounds is long-standing. Many Native tribes have a strong belief in powerful spirits and a particular interest in death, specifically the fate of the soul in the world of ghosts. Many Natives also believe that spirits coming back after death spell doom for the living and are to be avoided. There is a belief that when a person dies, a malignant influence is released and able to return to earth as a ghost. These spirits haunt burial grounds and might plague the living. Desecrating those burial grounds has preceded numerous reported instances of hauntings. In America, the revolutionary poet Philip Freneau believed these locations were mystical, sacred and filled with spirits that were still hunting, feasting and playing. Freneau wrote in his 1787 poem titled "The Indian Burying Ground":

> *Thou, stranger, that shalt come this way,*
> *No fraud upon the dead commit—*
> *Observe the swelling turf, and say*
> *They do not lie, but here they sit.*

CHAPTER 6

KALAMA, WASHINGTON

Where "Rail Meets Sail"

Next, we will explore the logging town of Kalama, Washington. Kalama was first settled by members of the Cowlitz Native American tribe. The first white settler, Ezra Meeker, settled here in 1853. In 1870, the Northern Pacific Railway built a headquarters and town here. General J.W. Sprague of the railway named the town in 1871 after the Native word *calama*, which means "pretty maiden." The town's motto was "Rail Meets Sail." Later, a ferry service was established that crossed the Columbia River.

The historic Montgomery House, built in 1908 as a private home, used to be a bed-and-breakfast. It also served at various times in its history as a bordello, a doctor's clinic whose operating room was located in the current dining area and a nine-room hospital. It is said that the land on which this structure was built was once a Cowlitz burial ground, and human bones have been unearthed here. The Cowlitz were decimated by smallpox, malaria and other diseases carried by white settlers, and it is said the Montgomery House is haunted by Native ghosts who died from these diseases. As described in the case of Mount Coffin, the belief in haunted Native burial grounds is long-standing.

At the secluded seven-acre Scaponia Park in nearby Scappoose, Oregon, the apparition of a man and his dog have been seen in the park. Legend says he is the ghost of a horse thief from the late 1800s. According to the story,

An old railway car, 2013. *Courtesy of lizzyliz, Pixabay.*

an angry mob caught the horse thief in his cabin located on the grounds, hanged him, shot his dog and buried them nearby.

No doubt Kalama has its fair share of haunted tales and mysterious activities.

CHAPTER 7

ST. HELENS, OREGON

"Halloweentown"

Continuing down the Columbia River, what is now the town of St. Helens was founded in 1845 by Captain Henry Montgomery Knighton, a native of New England, and named Plymouth after the location where the Pilgrims landed. The town name was changed to St. Helens in 1850 for its view of volcanic Mount St. Helens, thirty-nine miles away in Washington State. St. Helens, located in Columbia County, Oregon, is the county seat. This beautiful little town is located thirty minutes northwest of Portland on the Columbia River. However, despite its small-town charm, it is rumored to be one of the most haunted places in Oregon. Its nickname is "Halloweentown," in part due to four Disney movies of that name filmed and based here between 1998 and 2006.

One reportedly haunted site is the historic Klondike Bar and Restaurant in Olde Towne. Paranormal investigative teams have visited here and reported sensing that an altercation took place in the Victorian-era building's now-vacant second floor. They have also observed a coffee machine starting itself, as well as disembodied voices caught on digital recording machines. The ghost of a woman said to have suffered a miscarriage and who is searching for her baby is said to haunt the building. Visitors report the disembodied sounds of this searching, as well as mysterious voices.

At the historic Columbia Theatre, a grand movie palace built in 1928, employees and moviegoers claim to have witnessed mysterious activity. This includes the ghost of an elderly man reportedly seen sitting in one of the balcony seats, rocking back and forth.

Mount St. Helens, 2019. *Courtesy of debdenton, Pixabay.*

The ghost of an elderly man named George is rumored to be haunting the historic Kinder Cemetery. He is said to push or slap visitors and cause the temperature to rise when he is especially angry. One visitor to the cemetery described having an uneasy feeling, taking a photograph of a tree and seeing an elderly male apparition peeking out from behind the tree. They said they could sense the ghost creeping closer to them, and they departed as quickly as possible.

One former St. Helens resident reported that one night, when her husband went camping with friends and she was going to sleep, she heard voices whispering at the foot of her bed. She asked the voices to go to another room, as she was trying to sleep; the voices grew quiet. She also reported putting cookie sheets in the oven to keep them out of the way, and every night at exactly 11:30 p.m., they would "pop," seemingly from a temperature change.

St. Helens was the filming location of the Disney movie *Halloweentown* and its sequels, and the town embraces its haunted heritage. Haunted tours and ghost walks are conducted in the town throughout the month of October.

Next time you visit St. Helens, Oregon, keep an eye and ear out for strange sounds, sights and activities.

CHAPTER 8

FOREST GROVE, OREGON

Mysterious Masons

Twenty-five miles to the west of Portland is the city of Forest Grove. Prior to the 1840s, the Atfalati band of the Kalapuya Native American tribe lived here. After white settlers came to the area in the 1840s, it became known for farming. Forest Grove was the first city in Oregon's Washington County, being incorporated in 1872. In 1880, the Chemawa Indian School was established to forcibly assimilate Native American children. The Oregon Electric Railway began service in 1908, and the Southern Pacific Railway was established in 1914. The city is now part of the Greater Portland metropolitan area.

Forest Grove's Grand Lodge Hotel, with its striking white columns, was established in 1921 and for seventy-seven years was the Masonic and Eastern Star Home for aged and distressed Freemasons. In 1999, it was converted into the Grand Lodge Hotel. Freemasonry prides itself on being a system of morality, veiled in symbols, stories and pictures. The symbolism is primarily drawn from the stonemasons' tools used to build King Solomon's temple. These include the square, compass, level, trowel and others. King Solomon was the son of the biblical David, who served as the king of Israel from 970 to 931 BCE. Freemasons engage in rituals and rites of passage, through which they are initiated, pass, are raised and progress on their journey in the craft. There are three degrees of Freemasonry: Entered Apprentice, Fellowcraft and Master Mason. Masons are progressively taught the Masonic symbols and entrusted with grips, tokens, signs and words signifying to other Masons their level of degree. Symbols include the IOD, or All-Seeing Eye, which represents God and the Three Great Lights of Freemasonry: the Square, the Compass and the Book of the Law.

The Grand Lodge Hotel today is a popular ninety-room property used for weddings and conferences. However, there are also stories of haunted and paranormal activities at the hotel; a logbook is kept at the front desk in which guests and employees have described dozens of ghostly encounters.

Strange dried blood drops have been found on bedding and towels. Sleeping guests have awakened to find their blankets have been tucked in around them, as if an unseen nurse has cared for them. The scent of cigar smoke has been detected, although no one has been smoking. Guests have taken photographs of white, misty-looking orbs and have also reported showers and sinks gushing water, without anyone having turned them on. Guests and employees have also reported objects and furniture being rearranged by some unseen entity. One employee reported encountering the ghost of an old man wearing a gray-green cardigan and brown hat, as the hair on the back of her neck stood on end. She described how this figure watched her from below and how she could see right through the man, as if he were a spirit. She later recognized the man in an old photograph hanging on the lodge's second floor. The man, known as Old Joe, was said to be a former resident of the Masonic nursing home who was known to hide under the staircase and around corners, watching people, before his death. However, the lodge's most frequently reported ghost is a little old lady wearing glasses, nicknamed the Lavender Lady due to the scent of lavender flowers that accompanies her. There is a hand-painted image of her in room 232, on the back wall. She was first encountered in 1999 by construction workers who were converting the property into a hotel. They described the sudden scent of lavender wafting through the air. One worker described seeing a grinning, white-haired old woman; she seemingly meant no harm. Today, guests and staff still report scents of lavender lingering throughout parts of the lodge.

If you have the chance to visit or stay at Forest Grove's Grand Lodge, be on the lookout for strange, unexplainable sights and sounds.

CHAPTER 9

HAYDEN ISLAND, OREGON

Abandoned Amusements

In 1792, Hayden Island was discovered by the same Lieutenant William Robert Broughton, commander of the Royal Navy survey ship HMS *Chatham*, who named Mount Coffin in Longview, Washington. He named the island Menzies for the ship's botanist, Archibald Menzies. Lewis and Clark traveled through this area in 1805 and named the island Image Canoe Island after they discovered a large Native canoe with drawings of men and animals. The Chinook Native tribe laid the bones of their dead on open pyres and in canoes on Memaloose Island (now an Oregon state park) in the middle of the Columbia River. From the 1880s until the 1930s, the Chinook burial grounds were desecrated and the dead disturbed, perhaps leaving their spirits restless. The island was called Vancouver Island by Hudson's Bay Company. In the early 1800s, it was called Shaw Island after Colonel W. Shaw, who owned land there. It was renamed Hayden Island in 1851 for Oregon pioneer and early Vancouver settler Gay Hayden, who settled there and gained ownership of it. Hayden built a home and lived on the island for five years with his wife and children.

Hayden Island's Jantzen Beach was home to a sprawling 123-acre amusement park from the 1920s until 1970, nicknamed the "Coney Island of the West." After floods, a fire and an accidental death on the roller coaster, attendance at the park declined while property values in surrounding counties skyrocketed, forcing the park to close. The amusement park was dismantled, other than the 1921 C.W. Parker Carousel, which became part of the Jantzen Beach Shopping Center and is listed in the National Register of Historic Places.

An old carousel, 2016. *Courtesy of 165106, Pixabay.*

Hayden Island mist, 2017. *Courtesy of BicycleCurtis, Pixabay.*

Adults and children have witnessed two ghostly children, a little boy and girl, playing in the machinery room in the center of the ride, wearing 1920s-style clothing. It is not clear if tragedies, including those involving children, occurred at the former amusement park.

It is clear, based on witness reports, that ghostly spirits seem to be hanging on to this little-remembered piece of Pacific Northwest history. Maybe they are hoping to recapture the excitement of the many past amusements.

CHAPTER 10

PORTLAND, OREGON

Haunted City of Roses

Our next stop along the Columbia River is Portland, Oregon, the largest city we will explore. Portland was named in 2020 as the fifth most haunted city in America by *Travel and Leisure* magazine. Portland sits at the junction of the Columbia and Willamette Rivers, in the shadow of Mount Hood. It is nicknamed the "Rose City" and is blessed with both natural beauty and culture—though it may also be home to a number of haunted locations and personalities. Portland was one of the most dangerous port cities in the world at the turn of the twentieth century.

Like in much of the Pacific Northwest, Lewis and Clark's Corps of Discovery scouted the Oregon Country (as the region was known in the nineteenth century) in 1805 on behalf of President Thomas Jefferson. Interest in the region grew after the corps reported the mild climate, fertile land, green forests and many lakes and rivers located in the Pacific Northwest. In 1843, William Overton of Tennessee and his friend Massachusetts lawyer Asa Lovejoy floated down the Willamette River and discovered the area that would become Portland. Soon after they started to clear the land, Overton sold his share to Francis Pettygrove of Maine. In 1845, Lovejoy and Pettygrove flipped a coin to decide a name for the city. Pettygrove won and named the city after Portland, Maine. Portland grew quickly, especially after the Civil War, becoming a major port and shipping center.

Snaking under Portland's Chinatown are numerous "shanghai tunnels." The tunnels received their name either because they were built under Chinatown by Chinese workers or because China was the destination for

Mount Hood, 2018. *Courtesy of 26azr01, Pixabay.*

many kidnapped sailors. Countless men were illegally kidnapped (crimped) to serve unwillingly aboard ships. These tunnels ran from downtown bars and hotels to the waterfront along the Willamette River, and sailors were led through them to serve unwillingly on ships in need of crews. These men were drugged or knocked unconscious, waking up to find themselves aboard ships and out at sea. Women were likewise kidnapped and led to underground brothels, forced into prostitution or slavery. Opium dens, gambling houses and prisons were also said to be within the tunnels.

One haunted location is said to be Cathedral Park, the location of the 1949 murder of high school student Thelma Taylor. The park lies beneath the St. Johns Bridge in Portland, a dual suspension bridge patinaed in copper green, rising above the Willamette River. The park is named for the sweeping Gothic arches that form the supports for the bridge above. Views from the park capture the city's scenic beauty, the gently flowing river, the mountains and evergreens. Neighbors say you can still hear the screams of fifteen-year-old Thelma Taylor, a Roosevelt High School student. She was abducted from the park by twenty-two-year-old drifter Morris Leland while hitching a ride to a summer job. One week after Taylor's disappearance,

Leland was pulled over by police for stealing a car. He confessed to Taylor's murder at the police station and described the manner in which he murdered Taylor, placed driftwood over her body and wiped his fingerprints off her lunch pail. In 1951, Leland was tried for Taylor's murder, quickly found guilty and sentenced to death. After several unsuccessful appeals, in 1953 Leland was executed in Oregon's gas chamber. The stories about the crime are gruesome. One business owner reported that "he'd been down at the park at night and heard a girl scream 'help me, help me—somebody help me!'" It is said her spirit remains at the park where she was murdered.

Portland's Middle Eastern– and Spanish-style Bagdad Theater was lavishly built in 1927 by Universal Studios for $100,000 (over $1.5 million in 2021), with a $25,000 state-of-the-art organ. The theater was intended to host cinema and vaudeville acts. One ghostly story has it that a former stagehand, who longed to be an actor, hanged himself in the backstage area. Patrons have reported his spirit crossing in front of the screen and whispering behind it. A different ghost is reported to move around work papers and cleaning supplies in the theater. Employees have reported disembodied footsteps following them at night. Swinging doors have been observed opening and closing on their own in the kitchen.

An old Portland, Oregon bridge, 2016. *Courtesy of djkinney, Pixabay.*

The historic Columbia Pioneer Cemetery is located a mile south of the Columbia River and has been in use since 1857 as the final resting place for people from all classes and ethnic groups, well-known and everyday citizens. The cemetery was originally called the Love Cemetery for Captain Lewis Love, an early settler who lived on the land and made a living by transporting logs to Portland. The cemetery is the last resting place of founding fathers, pioneers and freed slaves who arrived along the Oregon Trail. The cemetery is said to be quite active in the supernatural sense. Thirteen-year-old John Mock drove oxen across the plains with his covered-wagon traveling pioneer family in 1852, from Missouri to Oregon. Later in life, he became one of Portland's leading citizens and lived in a beautiful Victorian home at University Park (Mock's Mansion, now a National Historic Landmark) until his death in 1916. He was a thirty-second-degree Freemason and served faithfully in offices of public trust. He is buried at the Columbian Pioneer Cemetery, and it is said that his spirit and those of several spectral children have been seen on the cemetery grounds.

The McMenamins Crystal Ballroom in Portland, built in 1914, was first named the Cotillion Hall, as it initially was used for the debutantes who were formally presented there. Formal debutante balls continued to be held there until after the Great Depression. It has since been used for rock-and-roll concerts, hosted other forms of music and been completely restored. The Crystal Ballroom is said to also be the home of a number of spirits. Staff and customers reported seeing apparitions dressed in 1920s-style clothing moving in and around the ballroom. One staff member reported witnessing a ghostly couple "jitterbugging" on the dance floor. These apparitions quickly evaporated from view. Another common occurrence in the main ballroom is the sound of disembodied dancers' footsteps and murmured conversation. According to local psychics, the bricks of the building hold the ghostly energy of past performers and dancers. One of the scariest encounters occurred after a live performance in the ballroom when a staff member heard the sounds of a child's laughter coming from behind one of the tables near the stage. When he went over to investigate, he felt a tug on his shirt. Startled, he turned swiftly around to find a small child staring up at him. The child almost immediately turned into mist and vanished. It has been reported that during performances, lights flicker on and off in one room but not in another. Other times, loud noises have reportedly been heard coming from the ballroom. When staff members investigate, the sounds abruptly stop. Guests have reported feeling ghostly fingers pulling on their clothing, hearing strange sounds and feeling cold spots—especially after performances. The Crystal Ballroom is said to be one of the most haunted places in Oregon.

The Heathman Hotel opened its doors in 1927 and was originally called the New Heathman. The Heathman is listed in the National Trust for Historic Preservation's Historic Hotels of America listing. There are over 260 trust member hotels in forty-four states, the District of Columbia, Puerto Rico and the U.S. Virgin Islands. Only hotels of historic significance, at least fifty years old and that have maintained their authenticity, sense of place and architectural integrity are listed. It is reported to have several haunted rooms. Screams have been heard by guests, emanating from rooms ending in the number 3. Room 703 is reportedly the most haunted in the hotel, with a guest purportedly jumping to their death from that room, falling through the glass window of the library below. In 2008, a guest staying in 703 went to the front desk and told staff that someone had thrown her room's clean towels on the floor. The staff promptly replaced her towels. Later, the woman noticed the new towels were also on the floor in the bathroom. She said she knew that no one else had been in the room. Also in 703, a guest taking a shower heard the TV in their room turn on. The guest went to investigate, turned off the TV and went back into the shower. The TV again turned itself on, and the guest complained to hotel staff. A staff member went to room 703 and turned the television on and off again; it seemed fine. Then, just as the staff member was leaving, the TV turned itself on again with the audio seemingly turned all the way up. The guest asked to be relocated to a different room. In room 503, guests reported a crying ghost waking them only to vanish when they got out of their beds. One woman staying in 503 complained to the manager that someone must have gone into her room without her permission. When the manager asked why she thought this, the woman explained that her suitcase and clothing had been moved about the room. The manager reviewed records and found no staff entered the room during that day. The night seemed to pass uneventfully; however, the next morning, the woman again complained that her clothing had been moved. In another incident, a hotel employee saw a giant ball of energy zipping about room 503. This became a regularly reported occurrence, and another cleaning staff member took a photo of it. The photo is said to hang in housekeeping's breakroom to this day.

The lovely Hollywood Theater, built in 1927 and since fully restored, originally hosted vaudeville shows and silent movies. Staff and patrons described weird sensations while inside the theater. Paranormal investigators and customers reported seeing and experiencing strange figures moving in and around the theater, including swirling lights, orbs, funnels, vortices and cold spots. One investigator reported that when she exited the women's bathroom, a swirling figure approached her and then abruptly vanished. Another paranormal researcher recorded the voice of Toby, said to be a "friendly spirit," who had been at the theater since the 1920s, when it first opened. The researcher reported that the spirit took on an orblike shape. Another investigator recorded a spirit named Steve as an electronic voice phenomenon, who indicated he liked to hide in the upstairs lobby area of the theater. He further said he had worked at the Hollywood most of his life until he became sick and passed away. He indicated he loved the theater and his job so much that he couldn't leave them, even after death. Another ghost reportedly smokes a cigarette and paces the halls of the theater. This female spirit taps customers and staff on the shoulder and then giggles and vanishes when they turn around.

The Roseland Theater was formerly a church, dating back to 1922. Prior to being renamed the Roseland Theater, it was known as Starry Night and hosted musical acts including Tina Turner and Mötley Crüe. It is reputedly haunted by Timothy Moreau, a twenty-one-year-old publicity agent and club promoter who was strangled and murdered there by the club's owner in 1990. It is said the murder was due to a counterfeit ticket scam gone wrong

Old theater seats, 2017. *Courtesy of coltsfan, Pixabay.*

and that Moreau's body was dumped in the Columbia Gorge some fifty-five miles away. Witnesses have reported hearing angry whispers in the hallways before and after screenings.

The North Portland Library dates back to May 1909, when it served as a reading room with about five hundred books. The library grew rapidly and opened a larger facility in 1913 and was again updated in 2000. Security cameras recorded the shadowy figure of an elderly man sitting in a chair in the second-floor conference room. Security staff had a strange, eerie feeling while viewing the figure. They went to investigate and reported the door swung open on its own when they reached for the doorknob—they found the room empty. When they returned to their workroom, they again saw the figure on the security screen. A Jefferson High School group of students working on a paranormal school project also visited the library and its upstairs bathroom and reported witnessing a ghost operating a hair dryer.

The beautiful Pittock Mansion, built in 1908, is allegedly haunted by its original owners, publishing magnate Henry Pittock and his wife, Georgiana, and their groundskeeper, all of whom died there. Visitors have reported the intense scent of rose perfume in the upper-floor rooms. They also reported disembodied footsteps, the sound of a shovel hitting the ground as if wielded by the groundskeeper, windows opening and closing on their own and a portrait of Henry Pittock moving on the wall on its own. Shadowy figures have also been observed moving furniture and house plants from room to room.

The University of Portland's Commons is said to be haunted by Frank Houston, who owned the property on which the Commons were built and refused to sell it to the university. His widow sold it to the school in the 1950s, which is when strange occurrences were first reported. Food service dish carts have been seen moving down the hall on their own, pots and pans have flown on their own off the walls, food and utensils have been thrown on the ground and a yelling voice has been heard. The university's Waldschmidt Hall is also said to be haunted by the ghost of former student Paul Hillgens, who drowned in the nearby Willamette River. His spirit, dressed in an old-fashioned bathing suit, wearing a baseball cap and sandals, has been seen walking the floors. When two security officers approached the figure and told him to "get out," he promptly disappeared.

At Reed College, reported hauntings date back to 1908 and include several ghosts on the third floor of the Prexy residence hall. It is thought these may be the spirits of students who lost their lives to drugs in the 1960s.

Tryon Creek State Natural Area is Portland's only state park, located along the Willamette River. Visitors have reported the sounds of ghostly horses whinnying, the disembodied voices of men talking and the sound of logging activities, even though the last major logging took place in the late 1800s.

In the middle of Forest Park in Portland is the Witch's Castle. Locals say the stone house dates back to the mid-1800s. Legend has it that a man named Danford Balch purchased land around the area and hired Mortimer Stump and his family to help clear the land. Stump and his family lived with the Balch family. Mortimer Stump, already married, and the Balches' daughter Anna fell in love, and Stump asked Balch if he could marry Anna. Balch refused, and Stump and Anna threatened to elope. An enraged Balch, said to have been "bewitched" by Stump's spurned wife, said he would murder Stump if he and Anna eloped. Stump and Anna, not heeding Balch's warning, eloped anyway in November 1858. When Stump and Anna later returned to Portland, Balch carried through with his threat and shot Stump in the face with a shotgun while they were all onboard the Stark Street ferryboat. In mid-October 1859, Balch became the first legally executed person in Oregon, hanged for his crime. Legend has it that the witch, Stump's wife, continued living in the stone house for some time. Unexplained supernatural activity is said to take place here and is attributed to the strange happenings that took place in the 1850s.

There is no shortage of haunted and supernatural sightings in Portland. No wonder it is thought to be one of the most haunted cities in America.

CHAPTER 11
STARVATION PASS

A Snowbound Train

The Pacific Express train departed The Dalles along the Columbia River on December 16, 1885, on its way to Portland. It had 148 passengers and crew aboard and only traveled about two miles before it ran into a twenty-five-foot-deep snowslide. There had been blizzards, high winds and heavy snowfall in the Columbia River Gorge, which also experienced avalanches. The train sat some fifty miles short of its destination of Portland.

Soon, the people on the train found that they were blocked from both the front and back, as snow piled up on the track. All on board, young and old, male and female, were asked to exit the train and begin to shovel. They shoveled for many hours, attempting to free the train from the snow and ice. Finally, the train's crew was able to back the train backward over a trestle.

However, the train was unable to continue its journey or return to The Dalles. The train carried little food or coal for its journey, and the people onboard wondered if they would have enough heat and food to survive the ordeal.

News of the crisis traveled fast and was reported on daily by the Portland *Morning Oregonian* newspaper. Some news stories were dramatically wrong, reporting that two passengers had starved to death and that smallpox had broken out on the train.

Over a dozen rescue train engines were dispatched and scattered along the tracks in an attempt to save the Pacific Express, its passengers and crew. Heavy snow continued to fall, the train's supply of coal was soon gone and the crew had to burn its wooden seat frames for heat.

A Washington blizzard, 2013. *Courtesy of 12019, Pixabay.*

With the food supply dwindling, the train conductor ordered most of the able-bodied men (about eighty) to walk to the destination of Portland, some fifty miles away. These men wrapped their feet in towels and exited the train into the blizzard. Most made it to Portland, while some stayed at Cascade Locks some eleven miles away. Others joined the eight hundred rescuers who were furiously digging the train out of the snow.

The train was trapped for twenty-one days, from December 16 to January 6, 1885, until rescue crews were finally able to free it. The Pacific Express, along with other trains that had been stuck at The Dalles, made their way to their destinations with over four hundred passengers and crew onboard. Although they had been cold, hungry and experienced illness, amazingly, no one died.

Photographer Carleton Watkins, on one of the relief trains from Portland, documented the harrowing events. He shared his thoughts on January 17, 1885, with the *Oregon Sentinel* newspaper, describing the train being stranded in forty-five-foot-deep snow in the Cascade Mountains. He expressed his hope that he could "teach others how much can be endured when a cracker is a blessing and a potato a luxury…when there is nothing warm among a hundred passengers excepting human sympathy, and nothing light but hope and a tallow candle."

Today, Starvation Pass is part of the state park aptly named Starvation Creek State Park, about eight miles west of Hood River in the Columbia River Gorge, with a spectacular 186-foot waterfall.

Ghosts are sometimes said to take the form of inanimate objects, including ghost trains and other vehicles believed to be controlled by the undead who, in life, were involved in accidents or wrecks or suffered other sudden and unexpected ends. Although no one was killed in the Starvation Pass incident, it was a traumatic event with lifelong consequences for those who experienced it. There is little doubt that this incident and the highly charged emotions that resulted added to the reported paranormal and supernatural climate within the Columbia River Gorge.

In some ways, this haunting, with no corresponding loss of life, is similar to that reported at Fort Stevens in Warrenton, Oregon. Although no lives were lost in either the Starvation Pass incident or the attack on Fort Stevens, the trauma of the events no doubt left an indelible mark on the people and the land.

CHAPTER 12

COLUMBIA RIVER GORGE AND HOOD RIVER

Ghosts in the Gorge

According to a 2020 issue of *Travel and Leisure* magazine, Portland is the fifth most haunted city in America. However, it seems some of these ghosts have left the city and taken up residence in the nearby Columbia River Gorge. The Gorge is a canyon and wonder of nature, stretching eighty miles long, and is at times four thousand feet deep. The Columbia River flows through and created the gorge. It forms the boundary between the states of Washington to the north and Oregon to the south. It is also reputed to be highly haunted.

Starting in Troutdale, on the western end of the Gorge, we encounter our first reported ghosts at McMenamins' Edgefield Inn. The McMenamin brothers—known for restoring and repurposing historic properties into hotels, restaurants and pubs—purchased the old Multnomah County Poor Farm and converted it into a destination resort. Built in 1911, the rambling brick structure served as home to the county's destitute, who, in turn, provided the labor to operate the surrounding three-hundred-acre farm.

It was a busy place during the Depression, but by the end of World War II, most residents were elderly, and it took on the role of a nursing home. The last patient left in 1982, and the place deteriorated over time, its future looking grim until the McMenamins arrived.

Today, it hosts a brewpub, winery, theater and restaurants and serves as a popular venue for weddings and concerts. The main building now serves as a hotel with a variety of rooms, from private suites to dorms.

The Columbia River Gorge, 2015. *Courtesy of imarketem, Pixabay.*

Guests have reported a number of ghostly experiences and sightings, including a woman reciting nursery rhymes in the early hours and a woman in white wandering the grounds. Guests report having their feet tickled and being serenaded by a flutist. Room 215 and the winery, located in the old infirmary, seem to house the most paranormal activity.

Continuing east along the Historic Columbia River Highway, we encounter the next reported ghost sighting. This historic road was built in 1913 to connect a series of waterfalls and stunning vistas along the Columbia River. Some have described it as one of the first scenic roads in America, combining traditional European and modern road building to create an amazing highway that blended well with the landscape. After a while, it was determined that a rest stop along the way would be very desirable, and plans were drawn for a modest wood and concrete structure on the promontory at Crown Point. However, Edgar Lazarus, a Portland architect, had other ideas and designed Vista House to be the remarkable German art nouveau masterpiece we know today. Volunteers have reported ghostly appearances by Lazarus. He apparently arrives in autumn and enjoys messing with the buttons on the elevator.

Vista House, 2015. *Courtesy of imarketem, Pixabay.*

The town of Hood River, originally established in 1858 as Dog River, is beautifully nestled along the Columbia River Gorge. It is home to wonderful outdoor activities, orchards and vineyards and sits at the foot of Oregon's tallest mountain, Mount Hood. The town also has an extensive and haunted history. The Lewis and Clark Expedition passed through this area on October 29, 1805. At that time, the area was inhabited by Natives, including a campsite called Waucoma, or "place of big trees." Hood River is home to two beautiful and historic hotels: the Hood River Hotel and the Columbia Gorge Hotel.

The current Hood River Hotel, the town's oldest still-operating hotel, was established in 1912 and is in the National Register of Historic Places. A prior hotel with that same name dates back to 1888 and was located near the train depot in the center of Hood River. Ola Bell was the original hotel owner, owning it for thirty years before her death in 1942. There are stories of Ola's ghost still inhabiting room 319 and haunting the hotel hallways. Guests and staff have heard and observed disembodied footsteps, doorknobs turning on their own and phantom phone calls. A guest who was staying in room 310 reported entering the room and immediately being overcome with a sense of dread. She wrote a review of the hotel, in which she said, "I nearly knocked my poor daughter down trying to get out. Every hair on my body stood on end, every rational thought left my brain and all I could do was yell GO GO GO GET OUT GET OUT."

The Columbia Gorge Hotel was constructed in 1921 by lumberman Simon Benson and replaced an earlier hotel built to serve passengers traveling the Columbia River on steamships. Benson was involved with the Columbia Gorge Scenic Highway and envisioned a hotel at the end of the highway. The current hotel was built on the site of the former 1904 Wah Gwin Hotel. Benson wanted to create a luxury property for the upscale motoring tourists visiting the Gorge, a "Waldorf of the West." The attractive Spanish and Mission-style structure was sited amid manicured gardens featuring a 208-foot waterfall and panoramic view of the river. Italian stonemasons who helped build the Columbia River Highway were enlisted to construct stone bridges and walls.

The hotel drew the likes of Presidents Franklin D. Roosevelt and Calvin Coolidge and top celebrities of the era, including Clara Bow, Myrna Loy, Rudolpf Valentino and Shirley Temple. However, the Depression brought hard times for Benson, and he sold the property to the Neighbors of Woodcraft, a fraternal order for lumber industry workers. It, in turn, operated the hotel for several decades as a retirement home for its members. In 1979, the building returned to its original use as a hotel and has undergone several renovations.

Staff and guests have reported unexplained fires, furniture and other objects moving on their own and vacant rooms being barricaded from the inside. The staff and guests have also reported the smell of cigar smoke with no identifiable source, said to be related to a retiree who died when the building was a retirement home. There have been observations of a man in a top hat and formal frock coat. A woman in white, who allegedly jumped from the hotel balcony, has been seen wandering the hotel and sitting on a park bench. A child's ghost has been seen lingering on the ground floor where a pool used to be. There have also been reports of a female ghost haunting room 330.

A 2020 hotel guest reported, "I saw a black mass hovering above my nightstand next to the bed."

A guest in 2018 said, "I saw a human form walk around the foot of our bed and to my side of the bed, suddenly I couldn't move or speak."

Another man in 2016 reported, "My wife said she couldn't move, speak or open her eyes, she was in a frozen state. I woke up when something felt like tugging or sitting on the blankets on my side of the bed that sent tingles up my legs."

Whatever the cause of these reported and unexplainable events, it is clear spirits may inhabit the Columbia River Gorge that are not planning on moving out anytime soon.

CHAPTER 13

HIJACKING AND AN AIRLINE DISASTER ABOVE THE COLUMBIA

THE GHOST OF D.B. COOPER

American folklore is full of stories about D.B. Cooper, who committed the United States' only unsolved hijacking. To this day, we do not know who Cooper is or was, where he came from or where he went. It is one of America's greatest mysteries, and it occurred over and adjacent to the Columbia River.

The day before Thanksgiving, November 24, 1971, a man in his mid-forties wearing dark sunglasses boarded a Northwest Orient airliner at Portland International Airport. His ticket was for a Dan Cooper, he sat in seat 18F and he almost immediately ordered a water with bourbon. Later, a law enforcement official erroneously referred to Cooper as "D.B.," and the abbreviation stuck.

Once the Boeing 727 was airborne, Cooper handed a flight attendant a note reading, "Miss, I've got a bomb, come sit next to me you're being hijacked."

Cooper opened his briefcase, which looked to contain an explosive, and then demanded $200,000 in cash and two parachutes. His demands were met upon landing at Seattle-Tacoma Airport, where he released passengers and two flight attendants.

Cooper then directed the pilot to take off again and fly at an altitude of ten thousand feet as the airliner made its way to Mexico City by way of Reno, Nevada.

A model of a Boeing 727, 2014. *Courtesy of aministracion, Pixabay.*

Forty minutes into this portion of the flight, a signal in the cockpit showed the plane's rear stairway had been lowered. The stairs were down, and two parachutes, the money and Cooper were all missing when the jet touched down in Reno. It is presumed Cooper parachuted out of the plane somewhere over the Oregon-Washington border, near Portland and the Columbia River.

A bundle of twenty-dollar bills was discovered by a child in 1980 when he was digging in the sandbar along the north bank of the Columbia River, west of Vancouver, Washington. The bills' serial numbers matched some of the ransom money. Law enforcement has Cooper's fingerprints from an in-flight magazine and DNA from the black tie Cooper was wearing before he jumped.

There have been numerous deathbed confessions and other claims of Cooper's discovery and/or copycat confessions of guilt. These include John List, a fugitive accused of murdering his family in New Jersey days before the hijacking; a man named Duane Weber who had been in prison near Seattle and told his wife in a 1995 deathbed confession that he was Cooper; and Kenneth Christiansan, a former paratrooper and employee of Northwest Orient airline. But to this day, Cooper's whereabouts remain unknown.

The FBI continues to follow up on leads in the case, with no clear end in sight. Law enforcement is literally chasing the "ghost" of D.B. Cooper, and it is difficult to predict the outcome of the search for the man some view as a modern-day Robin Hood.

An Airline Crash

On December 28, 1978, United Airlines flight 173, a DC-8 jetliner, crashed into a residential Portland, Oregon neighborhood near the intersection of East Burnside and 157th Avenue. The airplane had unbelievably run out of fuel.

Just prior to the crash, as the plane approached Portland, Captain Malburn McBroom pointed out the scenic sight of Mount Hood rising into view. He said into the intercom, "For you folks on the right side of the aircraft, there's a great view of the night skiing on the mountain out the window." Captain McBroom then prepared to release the landing gear on what had been a routine flight.

When the crew recognized the situation was dire, flight attendants gave the passengers orders to brace, putting their heads down ahead of the crash. Panic ensued, but passengers complied. A little over an hour later, the DC-8 fell out of the sky, out of gas, and ten passengers died. Observers said that when the plane hit the ground, buildings blocks away shook, and residents ran from their homes, offering help. The jetliner flattened two unoccupied houses and a group of trees before coming to a rest. The dead included four children, two crew members and four other passengers. It was a miracle that a greater number of deaths didn't occur.

The surviving passengers somehow managed to walk out of the debris, five of whom appeared at the doorstop of a neighboring house. Among the passengers who wandered off was an escapee from Oregon State Penitentiary whom police were returning to Oregon onboard the airliner. The prisoner's name was Kim Edward Campbell, and it was reported that he selflessly helped fellow survivors out of the crashed plane, but corrections officials said they "wish he hadn't then split like he did." Seven months later, Campbell was recaptured.

An investigation into the crash showed that Captain McBroom, his co-pilot and the flight engineer had become preoccupied with the airliner's landing gear, which was experiencing trouble. They lost track of the airplane's fuel load, which was exhausted, causing the crash.

Fortunately for all involved, Captain McBroom's flying skill (he was a former U.S. Navy pilot), the crew's training and good luck allowed for 175 of the passengers and crew to survive. According to the *Oregonian* newspaper, Multnomah County medical examiner William Brady had expected a much higher death toll and said he "began making plans to rent three large, refrigerated vans for storage of the expected large number of bodies."

A firetruck's emergency lights, 2021. *Courtesy of Marzahn Hellersdorf Live, Pixabay.*

Following the six-month investigation, the National Transportation Safety Board blamed pilot error for the crash. Other factors, according to author Julie Whipple in her 2018 book *Crash Course*, may have included poor airline maintenance practices.

In part, as a result of the investigation, commercial airlines instituted the NASA-created Cockpit Resource Management approach, which called for better communication between crew members. Although court hearings were held based on the crash, a jury ultimately found Captain McBroom was not responsible for any deliberate wrongdoing. United Airlines was cited for "wanton misconduct" over its maintenance practices.

On December 28, 1998, many survivors of flight 173 and their family members gathered in Portland for a twentieth-anniversary reunion of the crash. Captain McBroom, then seventy-two, attended, although he never got over the emotional toll the crash took. He said, "The fact that I lost some people and destroyed the airplane—it's painful." He later said that he had at one point considered suicide. Upon his being introduced at the reunion, those assembled wildly applauded. McBroom was said to be stunned by the audience's reaction, as they applauded McBroom's flying skill and diligence that saved so many lives. McBroom died six years later in 2004, at age seventy-seven.

As with other disasters, whether by ship, train or jetliner, the crash of United 173 no doubt left an indelible mark on the location into which it crashed. Such disasters and trauma are thought to fuel the paranormal activity of areas.

CHAPTER 14

BONNEVILLE DAM

A Project to Die For

Located some forty miles east of Portland, the Bonneville Dam is a work of engineering genius, controlling a flow of 1,200 gallons of water per second on the Columbia River between Oregon and Washington State. It is a national historic site and the largest supplier of electricity in the Pacific Northwest.

Construction started on the Bonneville Dam in 1934, and it was opened in 1937. Three thousand workers worked on it, with teams operating nonstop eight-hour shifts, twenty-four hours a day. A further four thousand employees in industries selling concrete, steel, lumber, generators and other materials needed for the dam were employed in support of the project. The arduous conditions that existed during the construction of the dam are reflected in the 1941 song "Jackhammer Blues" by folk singer Woody Guthrie. In the song, Guthrie describes the difficult nature of the work and the relief felt by the workers constructing the dam in surviving another day.

At the time of its opening, the dam was one of the most innovative, complex projects and the largest water project of its type in the United States. It had been proposed in 1929 by the U.S. Army Corps of Engineers and became a reality with the election of President Franklin Delano Roosevelt.

Workers came from many states, bringing their families in an attempt to escape the Great Depression. They were paid the high wage, for the time, of $0.50 per hour for unskilled laborers and up to $1.20 per hour for skilled workers.

Bonneville Dam, 2018. *Courtesy of sharonjoy17, Pixabay.*

The dam also has a darker side, having flooded a historic Native American village at Celilo Falls. A Native "ghost cult" on the Columbia River was said to exist in the nineteenth century. It is thought that this cult was formed in reaction to the incursion of white people and the resulting deaths of 90 percent of the Chinook Natives, killed between the 1770s and 1850. Along with other coastal tribes, the Chinook Natives were killed, in part, by diseases such as smallpox, malaria and measles. Bone carvings of human and animal figures with prominent ribcages were discovered in old burial pits, figures that the Natives believed represented death. Anthropologists have indicated there was an old Native belief in the impending destruction and renewal of the world—a belief that seemed to be confirmed by the tragic way and speed with which the Natives of the Lower Columbia Valley disappeared. The flooding of the Native American village at Celilo Falls could be seen as another step in the destruction of the Native cultures along the Columbia River.

Another part of the dark side of the Bonneville Dam relates to the death of twenty-six crew members who were killed during construction. Safety precautions were virtually nonexistent in the mid- to late 1930s. The government focused on efficiency and the successful completion of the project. This, in part, resulted in the deaths that occurred.

Finally, death has occurred related to terror threats that were made against the dam. The FBI shot and killed twenty-year-old Nathaniel Milligan on October 21, 1996, after a tape-recorded threat to blow up the dam in a $15,000 extortion attempt. Milligan was suspected of making the recorded threat on a tape recorder found near the dam's visitor center. It had a sign on it that read "play me" or "listen to this." He was shot twice and killed by an FBI agent as he approached authorities at the dam with a rifle in one hand and what he said was a detonator in the other. No explosives were found at the dam.

CHAPTER 15
STEVENSON, WASHINGTON, AND MULTNOMAH FALLS

A Jump from the Falls

The 620-foot-high natural wonder known as Multnomah Falls is one of the most photographed places in Oregon. It is located on Multnomah Creek in the Columbia River Gorge. Legend has it that this popular site is haunted by the spirit of a young Native American woman who died by suicide there.

The Multnomah are a tribe of Chinookan people who live in and around the Portland, Oregon area. At one time, Multnomah villages were located throughout the Portland basin and along the Columbia River. An old Multnomah legend tells of how the maiden leapt to her death from the Upper Falls in order to save her village from a plague and sickness. The legend says her ghost haunts the waterfall to this day. Some visitors have allegedly reported feeling the presence of the young woman at the falls in the winter or even seen her face appear within the white water.

It is said that the daughter of Chief Multnomah sacrificed herself to the Great Spirit from the top of Multnomah Falls. Tribes along the Columbia River had celebrated the marriage of the chief's daughter to a neighboring tribe member. The happiness didn't last long before an illness struck all the Native tribes along the river. The legend says the medicine man claimed the Great Spirit told him the entire tribe would die unless the Spirit received a sacrifice, the chief's daughter. The chief wouldn't allow it, but when his daughter saw the sickness affecting her loved ones, she voluntarily left in the middle of the night to go to the top of the cliff overlooking the Columbia River. She threw herself off the cliff. When the chief found his daughter's

Multnomah Falls, 2017. *Courtesy of 12019, Pixabay.*

body, he prayed to the Great Spirit for a sign that her spirit was well. The legend has it that, in a sign from the Great Spirit that the daughter's spirit was in fact well, water began pouring from the cliff, and the falls became known as Multnomah Falls.

Another Native legend that occurs near Stevenson, Washington, is the Bridge of the Gods over the Columbia River. Native folklore tells of a huge landslide some one thousand years ago that dammed the Columbia River, to be followed by the subsequent breaking away of part of the natural dam. A land bridge was left where the dam once stood. The Natives used this bridge until the great 1700 Cascadia earthquake that caused the bridge to fall into the water below.

As the Klickitat Natives tell the story, the Great Spirit had two warring sons: Pahto to the north of the river and Wy'east to the south. The Bridge of the Gods was created so that the family could visit each other, but the brothers fought over a woman named Loowit. Their anger shook the ground with fire, causing the bridge to fall into the water. Loowit could not choose between the two brothers, and it is said that she perished in the fighting. For punishment, the Great Spirit turned his sons into mountains—Pahto into Mount Adams and Wy'east into Mount Hood. Loowit became beautiful Mount St. Helens (which subsequently erupted in 1980).

Today, there is a modern steel Bridge of the Gods, over which the Pacific Crest Trail crosses between Oregon and Washington, through the Columbia River Gorge. The Pacific Crest Trail extends over the Cascades and Sierra Nevada Ranges from the Canadian to the Mexican border.

CHAPTER 16
MOUNT HOOD

"Heeeere's the *Shining* Hotel!"

When film director Stanley Kubrick was looking for the perfect stand-in for the fictional Colorado-based Overlook Hotel in *The Shining*, the unique 1930s Timberline Lodge in Government Camp, Oregon, on top of Mount Hood, is what he chose for the movie's exterior scenes. Kubrick even brought in *The Shining* author Stephen King to secure his approval of the location. Mount Hood lies just south of Stevenson, Washington, and the Columbia River.

More than one million people visit the lodge annually. It is designated as a National Historic Landmark and is very impressive, with its imposing stone masonry, hand-carved beams, pitched roof and snowy mountaintop setting. Visitors wander and explore the dozens of unique rooms with handmade furniture and carved beams. The lodge also contains Oregon's most iconic bar, the Blue Ox, hidden away behind the main lobby. While there is no hedge maze as existed in the movie, it does not take much imagination to remember actor Scatman Crothers driving his snowcat-type vehicle around the lodge's grounds.

One of the most memorable haunted rooms from the movie is room 237 (it was 217 in the book but switched to the imaginary 237 so as to not scare off guests from the actual 217). A Mrs. Massey died in room 237 and was the lodge's most recent death prior to Jack Nicholson's movie family the Torrances moving in. She died by suicide in the bathroom of room 237 and is said to have since become a zombie-like creature that seduces boys and young men and attempts to kill them.

Mount Hood, Oregon, 2016. *Courtesy of 12019, Pixabay.*

A ghost hunter who visited the lodge stayed in a nearby room and reported hearing footsteps and whispers coming from the hallway throughout the night.

CHAPTER 17

THE DALLES

Poisoning on the River

Bhagwan Shree Rajneesh was a spiritual leader with a significant international following. In 1981, Rajneesh decided to relocate to the United States and chose, with his chief of staff Ma Anand Sheela, the sixty-four-thousand-acre Muddy Ranch in Oregon's Wasco County, near The Dalles along the Columbia River.

The new settlement at Muddy Ranch soon had about seven thousand residents, all followers of Rajneesh, who made efforts to keep the press out. Rajneesh famously displayed dozens of Rolls-Royce automobiles that he fancied and kept. Some of his followers openly carried weapons. In 1982, after a number of Rajneesh's followers moved to the tiny town of Antelope, eighteen miles from the ranch, they began to call that town Rajneesh and attempted to incorporate it as the city of Rajneeshpuram. The State of Oregon fought the creation of this new city as illegal due to it being closed to non-adherents. The Rajneeshees tried to expand their voter base by moving homeless people into the area.

In 1984, Wasco County commissioner Bill Hulse and others who toured the ranch were poisoned by Rajneeshees, who put bacteria into their drinking water. The Rajneeshees denied doing this until 1985, when they admitted it was done as revenge for the county's redistricting efforts. Chief of Staff Ma Anand Sheela made it known that the guru wanted his people to serve on the county's board of commissioners and was frustrated at the county's efforts to stop this from occurring.

Shaniko, Oregon, in Wasco County, Oregon, south of the Columbia River, 2013. *Courtesy of ljlabarthe, Pixabay.*

In September 1985, Ma Anand Sheela and other Rajneesh leaders left Rajneeshpuram after they were accused of a number of crimes. Specifically, they were accused of arson, wiretapping, attempted murder and planting salmonella bacteria in the salad bars of several area restaurants (some 750 people were sickened).

Rajneesh denounced Sheela and left the area by chartered airplane in October 1985. He later made a plea bargain on immigration fraud charges and agreed to leave the United States.

Rajneeshpuram became a ghost town.

Traumatic events, whether or not they involve death, have been reported to result in supernatural and paranormal events and spirits. No doubt this disturbing chapter that occurred along the Columbia River has had an impact on the reported presence of ghosts.

CHAPTER 18

INLAND SHIPWRECKS
ON THE COLUMBIA

In *Haunted Graveyard of the Pacific*, I focused on the many hauntings at the mouth of the Columbia River, where it meets the Pacific Ocean and the coastal areas between Portland, Oregon, and Seattle, Washington. In addition to the reported land-based hauntings, I explored the many shipwrecks stretching along the Pacific Northwest coast, from Tillamook Bay in Oregon, past the treacherous Columbia Bar near Astoria, up the Washington coast, the Juan de Fuca strait separating Canada from the United States and up the western coast of Vancouver Island. Here, we will explore shipwrecks farther inland on the Columbia River and its tributaries.

Columbia River steamboats wrecked for a variety of reasons, the most common of which was colliding with other boats, rocks and logs. Other reasons included fires, boiler explosions, punctures of the hull or ice on the waterway.

The *Oregona* hit an anchored barge on the Willamette River on December 26, 1913, and sank. On December 30, 1907, the *Annie Comings* sank near St. Johns, Oregon (two miles downstream from Portland on the Willamette River), within three minutes of being struck by the barque *Europe*. Fortunately, no one was injured. The *Clatsop Chief* collided with the steamship *Oregon* on February 28, 1881, and sunk, losing four people to drowning. The *F.B. Jones* was rammed and sunk by the tanker *Asuncion* in 1907 on the Columbia River. The *Daisy Ainsworth* hit a rock and sank in bad weather, just above the Upper Cascades in Washington on November

An old steamboat, 1912. *Courtesy of WikiImages, Pixabay.*

22, 1876. The *Harvest Queen*, a larger boat that weighed 846 tons and was two hundred feet long, struck a fish trap piling on November 19, 1896, and sank. The *Oregon* hit debris (logs or another obstruction) on the Willamette in 1854, was bumped loose by the *Gazelle* and sank. Later, the *Gazelle* blew up on the river in 1854, with at least twenty people killed instantly—four died later—and a number injured. A number of those killed on the *Gazelle* were buried in Portland's Lone Fir Cemetery, which is reportedly haunted. The *Orient* hit a rock on the Cowlitz tributary in Washington in 1894 and burned. On February 8, 1906, the sternwheeler *Dalles City* sank after hitting a rock in the upper Columbia River. The *Madeline* hit a snag on the Cowlitz River, a tributary of the Columbia River, and sank on March 23, 1925. The *Diamond O.* struck a bridge at Vancouver, Washington, rolled over and sank on April 25, 1934.

Boiler explosions were a less common way shipwrecks occurred, but they did happen. On August 8, 1853, the *Canemah* was the first Oregon steamboat to suffer a boiler explosion, while sailing on the Willamette River. One passenger was killed, but the boat survived. In May 1853, at the Willamette River's Rock Island, the *Shoalwater*'s boiler exploded. There were no deaths, and the ship was rebuilt as the *Fenix*. As mentioned, the *Gazelle* exploded on April 8, 1854, resulting in a great loss of life. On May 6, 1875, the *Senator* blew up at the dock in Portland, severing the mooring lines and causing the wreck to drift downriver and wash up at the historic town of Albina, Oregon (now part of Portland). On January 18, 1912, the *Sarah Dixon* exploded near the town of Kalama, Washington, near Longview, killing its captain, first mate and fireman. In 1943, the *Cascades* exploded and burned in Portland.

The *Telephone*, one of the fastest ships on the lower Columbia River, burned near Astoria in November 1887, with 140 passengers and 32 crew on board. The Astoria fire department arrived on the scene and saved the *Telephone*, allowing it to be rebuilt and placed back into service. The *J.N. Teal* burned near Portland on October 22, 1907. The *James Clinton* was destroyed near Oregon City on April 23, 1861, after it was ignited by sparks from burning buildings across the river. On several occasions, there were instances of more than one steamboat destroyed by fire in the same incident, always while moored together. On July 7, 1915, in Wenatchee, Washington, there was a terrible fire. Most of the Columbia and Okanogan Steamboat Company's ships were moored together at a riverbank barge. The *Chelan*, *Columbia*, *North Star* and *Okanogan* were engulfed in flames sometime after 11:00 p.m., with all destroyed. Arson was suspected, but no responsible party was ever found. The fire, together with the company's ship *Enterprise* later sinking, resulted in the Columbia and Okanogan going out of business.

The *Portland* was swept over Willamette Falls on March 17, 1857, and destroyed, killing its captain and two others. The *E.N. Cooke* was lost in the Clackamas Rapids, just north of Oregon City. In 1905, at the Entiat Rapids, a tributary of the Columbia River near the town of Entiat, Washington, the *Alexander Griggs* was wrecked. On May 15, 1906, the *Selkirk* was wrecked at the Rock Island Rapids on the Willamette River. In 1933, at Three Mile Rapids on the Columbia River near Dalles, Washington, the *Hercules* was wrecked.

Powerful floods could overwhelm a steamboat and carry it out of control into a riverbank, rock or other obstruction. The *Georgie Burton* experienced this in 1948 at the lower end of the former Celilo Canal, a canal connecting two points of the Columbia River between Oregon and Washington east of the Dalles, which was flooded following completion of the Dalles Dam in 1957.

The U.S. Army Corps of Engineers sternwheeler *Asotin* was crushed in the ice on the Columbia River near Arlington, Oregon, in 1915.

The *Bonita* was driven onto a rock in the Columbia Gorge by a gale on December 7, 1892. Also in the Gorge, the *Dalles City* was driven ashore by a sandstorm near Stevenson, Washington, along the Columbia River, on September 14, 1912. It was said that a severe, hurricane-like storm destroyed the *J.D. Farrell* in Jennings Canyon in June 1898. The *Oakland* was overcome by high winds on Upper Klamath Lake on October 6, 1912. The *Cowlitz*, proceeding downriver from the Dalles in September 1931, was swamped by high winds and waves.

These disasters, although fewer than the two thousand ships and countless lives lost in the Graveyard of the Pacific, had a significant impact on the reported paranormal and supernatural environment of the region.

CHAPTER 19

THE TRI-CITY AREA

Nuclear Fallout and Apparitions

Continuing east, the Tri-City area, where the Yakima, Snake and Columbia Rivers connect in the Columbia Basin of eastern Washington, is made up primarily of three closely linked cities.

Hanford, Washington, was a small agricultural community that was condemned by the federal government and depopulated in 1943 to make room for the nuclear production facility known as the Hanford Site. The site sits alongside the Columbia River and was one of the major spots of nuclear production during the Cold War. The river water was used to cool its reactors, and consequently, much of the waste was vented into the Columbia River through contaminated groundwater. In the 1990s, radioactive waste was found in fish that was being eaten by locals, and the waste itself was found as far as two hundred miles downstream, all the way to the Pacific coast. This spawned one of the biggest cleanup efforts in American history, which continues to this day. The sickness caused to the local fish and its negative impact on the local population is reminiscent of the fishborne illnesses in La Push, Washington, on the Pacific coast. In that case, and as described by an elderly Squamish Native man in the 1890s, locally caught salmon were found to be covered in sores and blotches and unfit for consumption. However, because his people depended on the fish, they continued to catch and store the salmon for the winter's food supply and eventually ate it. The Natives became very sick as a horrible skin disease broke out; none were spared. Men, women and children died in agony by the hundreds. When spring arrived and fresh food was finally available, there were hardly any

The Columbia River, 2010. *Courtesy of ArtTower, Pixabay.*

Natives left. It was reported that the level of mortality was so great that it was impossible for the survivors to bury their dead. Rather, they simply pulled the houses down over the bodies and left them there. As we have seen, tragedies like this tend to result in increased paranormal activity. These types of disasters, whether natural or, as in this case, by man's experimentation with nuclear energy, scar the land and environment and are said to have supernatural ramifications.

Pendleton, Washington, began as a commercial center in 1851 with the establishment of a trading post. The town was named for politician and diplomat George H. Pendleton, who served as a U.S. representative and senator from Ohio from 1885 to 1889 and ran as the vice presidential candidate with Democrat and former Union general George B. McClellan against Republicans Abraham Lincoln and Andrew Johnson (the Democrats lost).

The historic Renaissance Revival–style 1915 Umatilla County Library building was funded by steel tycoon Andrew Carnegie. It served as the county library and then as the Pendleton Public Library until 1996, before it was listed in the National Register of Historic Places in 1997. It is now home to the Pendleton Arts Center. The ghost of a librarian named Ruth, who is said to have died by eating lye soap in the basement, haunts the building. Witnesses have reported the ghost moving objects around in the building and hearing disembodied footsteps, and a female spirit has been seen staring at people from the building's windows at night. Pendleton has a downtown underground made up of tunnels in the town's former red-light district, where businesses operated in the early 1900s. One of these passageways is said to have been the living quarters for Chinese immigrants and is reportedly haunted.

At the Red Lion Hotel, the ghost of a 2006 suicide victim and former employee is rumored to be present. This spirit has been seen and blamed with tinkering with appliances, playing pranks and walking down the hotel's halls.

The Eastern Oregon Correctional Institution was originally built in 1913 as the Eastern Oregon State Hospital for long-term mental patients. It was converted into a prison in 1983. Prison guards have reported hearing disembodied cries for help inside prison cells.

In the hills outside the eastern Washington city of Kennewick and located along the Columbia River, the "Baby Graves" is a private graveyard that holds the bodies of deceased babies (no adults). It has been reported that late at night, you can hear the sounds of babies crying.

The eastern Washington city of Richland, just north of Kennewick along the Columbia River, was previously the site of the Native American village of Chemna, which stood for centuries at the mouth of the Yakima River. In 1910, the city was incorporated and named for Nelson Rich, a state legislator and land developer. In the 1940s, the U.S. Army turned the area into a bedroom community for workers on the top-secret nuclear Manhattan Project at the nearby Hanford Site. Monterosso's is a Richland Italian restaurant that opened in 1995 and is housed in a converted 1947 Pullman railcar (what a cool idea!). Some employees believe it is haunted. There are reports of a shadowy figure at the back table, unexplainable noises, doors opening and closing on their own, music suddenly blasting from a stereo and lids flying in the kitchen. On one occasion, a new employee yelled from the restroom in the back of the train car that a phantom handprint had appeared on the stainless-steel walls of the restroom that had just been scrubbed, only to vanish a few moments later. Some reported feeling a friendly "presence" in the railcar. On another occasion, an oven stopped working for no reason. Employees later discovered it had been inexplicably unplugged, but not by any of the employees. The railcar had previously been used as a tailor shop from 1979 until 1994 by a man who collected old cars. Prior to that, it was used as a dining car on the Northern Pacific Railway, traveling on the East and West Coasts.

Native Americans have lived in the Umatilla, Oregon area along the Columbia River for thousands of years, fishing the nearby waters. The Lewis and Clark Expedition journeyed through this area and made note of the villages. The first post office was established in 1851, and the Umatilla Indian Reservation was created in 1855. In 1862, after gold had been discovered in Idaho and Montana, the Columbia River became an important passageway to the gold fields, and the area grew. Umatilla became an important trade and distribution center for gold miners, farmers and ranchers. The town was dismantled in the mid-1960s when it was feared the John Day Dam would cause flooding and was rebuilt south of the original town. In July and August 2013, an investigation was conducted into a house in Umatilla. The homeowner had reported strange occurrences at the house, including heating turning itself on and off and doors opening and windows closing seemingly on their own with no explanation. The ghost investigators set up their equipment, and a short time later, they noted their flashlight began turning itself on and off. Later, a motion sensor upstairs in the house began to flash, even though no one was present. After midnight, the system showed one of the cameras in an upstairs bedroom had been bumped by something, even though no one was there. The investigators concluded that while some of these events could be explained by cars driving by and other reasons, there could be paranormal activity at the house.

In Prosser, Washington, about twenty-eight miles from Umatilla, St. Matthew's Episcopal Church has been serving the community since 1907. It was featured in an episode of television's *Ghost Hunters*, in which witnesses reported the apparition of a small boy, a size-six footprint that seemed to come from nowhere and the smell of burning wood.

People say the Capital Theater in Yakima, Washington (in central Washington), is haunted by a friendly ghost who made itself known during a late-night clean-up. They say he is friendly but very mischievous. The theater opened on April 5, 1920; it was severely damaged by fire in 1975, painstakingly restored to its original state and reopened in 1978.

The 1905 Bridge Creek Flora Inn in Fossil, Oregon (south-central Oregon, south of the Columbia River), originally built as a homestead, is said to be haunted by a woman and man who, because they could not be together in life, killed themselves so they could presumably be together in death. It is said the young woman was upset she could not marry her rich farmer lover and jumped from the third story of the inn. The farmer then hanged himself from a tree in front of the inn. People have reported seeing a man hanging at night and hearing the sounds of unseen horses.

Not far from the Tri-Cities area is Finley, Washington, founded in 1906 and named for pioneer settler George E. Finley. A boy named Adam is said

The Yakima Valley, Washington, 2021. *Courtesy of 15414483, Pixabay.*

to have drowned in the Columbia River near Finley. Adam's parents were so distraught, they would go to the riverbank and talk with their son's spirit. They said Adam would reply to them with loud bursts of water. After Adam's parents passed away, local residents would go down near the riverbank on Yew Road's levy and talk with the "Finley Ghost." Legend has it that when you toss a rock into the Columbia River, the Finley Ghost wakes up and lets you know of his presence.

There is no doubt the Tri-Cities area has its fair share of reported ghostly activities.

CHAPTER 20

WENATCHEE AND LEAVENWORTH, WASHINGTON

Bavarian Poltergeists

T he city of Wenatchee was named for the nearby Wenatchi Native tribe. The name Wenatchee means "river which comes from canyons," as it is located at the confluence of the Columbia and Wenatchee Rivers. The city has two nicknames: the Apple Capital of the World, due to the area's many orchards, and the Power Belt of the Great Northwest, for the hydroelectric dams on the Columbia River. The village of Nikwikwi'estku was a fishing camp prior to the arrival of white settlers. In 1811, surveyor David Thompson met Native tribe members at Wenatchee and was invited into the village; fur traders reported friendly relations through the mid-1800s. A smallpox epidemic occurred in 1817, as well as food shortages in 1841. The U.S. Army intervened in 1856, stopping a possible alliance between the Yakama and Wanatchi tribes and forcing the Wenatchi to engage in a five-mile-long march. Roman Catholic priests performed missionary work in the area from the 1860s to the 1890s. Wenatchee was incorporated as a city on January 7, 1893. Today, the city is the largest city and county seat of Chelan County, with over thirty-four thousand residents. Wenatchee and neighboring towns have haunted tales to tell.

The IvyWild Inn in Wenatchee is a Tudor-style historic home that was formerly the Cherub Bed and Breakfast Inn. Legend has it that a man who was away for business returned and found his wife being unfaithful there. It is said the man killed his wife's lover in the house, on the stairs. Visitors have reported hearing the sound of the disembodied footsteps

The nearby town of Cashmere, Washington, 2014. *Courtesy of donwhite84, Pixabay.*

of the husband walking up and down the steps. They have also reported bloodstains on the stairs. Some longtime Wenatchee residents insist the tale is false, made up to scare children.

To the east of Wenatchee, in 1889, the town of Govan was established as a depot for the Central Washington Railroad line. Inside the depot, the post office was established that same year. In 1890, a large sand bank was discovered, and railroad contractor Wood, Larson and Company made Govan its headquarters. At its peak in 1889, Govan had some one hundred residents who were primarily employed moving sand for the railroad. The town became a point on the railroad for loading grain and fruit grown in the region onto trains bound for Spokane, Washington. By 1909, Govan was booming with two churches, a hotel, general stores, a drugstore, a bank, a school and a saloon. Several unsolved murders occurred in Govan. In 1902, Judge J.A. Lewis (who was known to keep large sums of cash in his home) and his wife were murdered. The perpetrator killed Judge Lewis with an axe and beat his wife to death behind their barn. In the spring of 1903, a masked gunman entered the Govan Saloon and killed resident C.S. Thennes. The murderer was caught but inexplicably not convicted. Govan's final murder victim was Lillie Lesnew in 1941; her body was found at her farm, and her son Wes had disappeared. Wes's skeleton was discovered by a rider on horseback in 1948. The case was never solved. Today, Govan is a ghost town, with its remaining structures a modern grain elevator used during harvests and the old abandoned schoolhouse.

A horse-drawn carriage in Leavenworth, Washington, 2020. *Courtesy of 1004us, Pixabay.*

The city of Leavenworth lies to the west of Wenatchee, along the Wenatchee River, a tributary of the Columbia River, and has a fascinating history. The Great Northern Railway had a regional headquarters there in the early 1900s (it later moved to Wenatchee). The town was once a center for logging. It experienced hard times throughout the first half of the twentieth century. In 1962, Project LIFE (Leavenworth Improvement for Everyone) was initiated in partnership with the University of Washington. It looked into ways to revitalize the economy. Two Seattle businessmen, Ted Price and Bob Rodgers, who had bought an area failing café, came up with the idea of modeling and converting the town into a Bavarian-style city, with the Cascade Mountains serving as the Alps. They visited the California town of Solvang, itself modeled on small Danish towns, to serve as an inspiration. Today, the town is a major tourist destination. Stories and tales of the spirits of early pioneers and adventurers roaming the town's streets have been reported. One story is about Chas Gordon, a Leavenworth businessman whose murder some one hundred years ago has never been solved. It is said his ghost still haunts the area where he once did business. The Tumwater Inn, once a thriving saloon in the 1940s to 1960s where people came to dance, is said to have a spirit that plays old-time tunes on an invisible piano. The Tumwater closed its doors in 2017. Disembodied sobs have been reported emanating from Thorp Cemetery, between Leavenworth and Ellensburg,

Washington, where the dead do not seem to be resting in peace. Finally, there have been legends about gold mines in the area for more than one hundred years. One legend centers on Ingalls Creek, where it is said gold was once found in the 1860s and 1870s, but none since 1872. Some have speculated that the earthquake of 1872 damaged the mountains and creek, resulting in the disappearance of the gold. However, tales continue of ghostly gold miners continuing to search.

The Original Cascade Tunnel, near the town of Wellington to the west of Leavenworth, was created in 1900 for railway travel to avoid Steven's Pass's steep switchbacks. The 2.6-mile Cascade Tunnel was, at the time, a feat of engineering. Wellington was a railway stop located on the west entrance of the tunnel. An avalanche occurred here in 1910, claiming nearly one hundred lives. Snow fourteen feet high wiped out two passenger trains that had been stranded at the depot. Observers have reported disembodied voices in the area, along with a sense of dread. It was the deadliest avalanche in U.S. history.

The New Cascade Tunnel, opened in 1929, stretches for eight miles through the mountain underneath Steven's Pass. The exhaust from passing diesel engine trains has been so bad, as has ventilation in the tunnel, that crews have to wear respirators to breathe in oxygen. Built inside the tunnel are a number of emergency stations. The health ramifications of the train exhaust, together with the fatalities that have occurred, have resulted in lawsuits.

The city of Snohomish, with a population of about ten thousand, sits adjacent to the Snohomish River and to the west of Wenatchee and the other towns just mentioned. It was founded in 1859 by pioneer E.F. Cady. It served as the Snohomish County seat from 1861 to 1897, when it was relocated to Everett. Its downtown area is in the National Register of Historic Places and is home to a number of antique stores. The Oxford Saloon was built in 1900 as a dry goods store and now serves as a restaurant. There was a great deal of violence that occurred there when it was a saloon. Visitors and employees have reported ghostly shadow figures and mysterious incidents, including the spirit of a policeman who was killed while working on his off hours as a bouncer at the saloon. Investigators visited the saloon in 2005 and 2006 and detected voice phenomena and other anomalies that appeared to take human form when photographs were produced.

The Cabbage Patch restaurant in Snohomish has been described as a great place to eat, with an old-timey feel and a fireside lounge. Paranormal activity has been reported, including witnesses reporting the ghost of a young girl looking out the upstairs windows and standing on the stairs. Also reported have been dishes moving and breaking on their own and drinking glasses being rattled by a disembodied source.

To the south of Leavenworth, in the foothills of the Wenatchee Mountains, the mining town of Blewett was established in the 1890s. It was created as part of the mining boom and was known as violent and chaotic. From the 1890s until 1910, when the veins of ore were exhausted, the town had a hotel, school, blacksmith, saloon, assay office and miners' cabins. Having experienced abandonment, isolation and fires, all that remain of Blewett are the mine entrances and the foundation of the old stamp mill.

The ghost town of Liberty, to the south of Leavenworth, sprang up in the 1870s with the discovery of gold. Originally called Meaghersville after local miner Thomas Meagher, it was the oldest mining town in Washington State. Today, some of the structures as well as the mine can be found. Liberty is still inhabited. There are legends and tales of the original miners' spirits' presence.

To the southwest of Leavenworth is the historic town of Roslyn. The Brick Saloon, built in 1889, is said to have great food and is famous as the setting for the 1990s television series *Northern Exposure* and the 1979 film *Runner Stumbles*. It is also known for its reported hauntings. Brick employees and customers have reported the ghosts of a little girl and a cowboy, as well as the disembodied playing of the piano in the back room. The Roslyn Cemetery, established in 1886, holds twenty-five separate cemeteries containing five thousand graves. It is said that many of those killed in Roslyn's mine accidents are buried in the cemetery.

Farther to the west of Roslyn lies Franklin, Washington. It was established in the 1880s as a coal mining town, and repeated crises and deaths soon occurred. Local miners went on strike, and the mines invited African American workers from Missouri, Illinois, Kentucky and Tennessee to take their place, with offers of good pay and free transportation. The local miners became upset, and a riot broke out. Two people were killed before the Washington National Guard restored order. In 1894, one of the worst American mining disasters occurred when thirty-seven miners tragically suffocated to death due to a fire in the mine that appeared to have been intentionally started. The mine ceased to function in 1919, and the town became a ghost town. Some of Franklin's remnants remain, including a cemetery.

There is no doubt that Wenatchee, Leavenworth and other nearby towns have their fair share of reported spirits, paranormal and other supernatural activity.

CHAPTER 21

GRAND COULEE DAM

Electric City Phantoms

The Grand Coulee Dam, like the Bonneville Dam, is a work of engineering genius. It is a concrete gravity dam on the Columbia River in Washington State. It was constructed between 1933 and 1942 by some eight thousand workers (as compared to three thousand workers for Bonneville). The dam's purpose is to produce hydroelectric power and provide irrigation water. Franklin Delano Roosevelt presided over the dam's authorization and completion, and a reservoir created by the dam, along the Columbia River, is called the Franklin Delano Roosevelt Lake. The Northwest United States' growing industries relied on the dam for power during World War II.

Seventy-seven men were killed during the construction of the dam. An additional four men were killed during the construction of the Nathaniel Washington Power Plant and Forebay Dam, part of the Grand Coulee, from 1967 to 1975. This compares to the death of twenty-six crew members in the construction of the Bonneville Dam. A question that is sometimes raised about dams during the building of which workers died is whether there are bodies buried in the concrete. There is no evidence of this with either the Grand Coulee or Bonneville Dam. As mentioned earlier, safety precautions were virtually nonexistent in the 1930s. The government focused on efficiency and the successful completion of the project. This, in part, resulted in the deaths that occurred.

Approximately three thousand Native people who had lived near the present-day Grand Coulee Dam for hundreds of years were forced to

The Grand Coulee Dam, 2021. *Courtesy of tegawi, Pixabay.*

relocate due to the large construction project. The Natives' ancestral lands were partially flooded with the creation of the Grand Coulee and reservoir. Towns such as Inchelium, home to 250 Coleville Natives, were submerged and relocated. Kettle Falls, at one time a Native fishing ground, was inundated. An event called the Ceremony of Tears was held over three days in June 1940 by the Confederated Tribes of the Colville Reservation to mark the end of fishing at Kettle Falls. Other villages as well as old Native burial grounds were displaced. In September 1939, a burial relocation project was started in which human remains were placed into small containers. The manner of collection destroyed archaeological evidence of the Natives' presence, although many artifacts were found. The exact number of graves relocated in 1939 varies greatly depending on who reported it. The Bureau of Reclamation reported 915 graves and field workers reported 1,388 graves, while Native leaders reported 2,000 graves. By 1940, the Bureau of Reclamation had stopped grave relocation, and the additional burial sites were covered by water.

As described earlier, the belief in haunted Native burial grounds is long-standing. Many Native tribes have a strong belief in powerful spirits and a particular interest in death, specifically the fate of the soul in the world of ghosts. Many Natives also believe that spirits coming back after death spell doom for the living and are to be avoided. There is a belief that when a person dies, a "malignant influence" is released and able to return to earth as a ghost. These spirits haunt burial grounds and may plague the living. Desecrating those burial grounds has preceded numerous reported instances of hauntings.

Also as described earlier, a Native "ghost cult" on the Columbia River was said to exist in the nineteenth century. It is thought that this cult was formed in reaction to the incursion of white people and the resulting deaths of 90 percent of the Chinook Natives, killed between the 1770s and 1850. Along with other coastal tribes, the Chinook Natives were killed, in part, due to diseases such as smallpox, malaria and measles. The flooding of the Native American villages and the displacement of burial grounds could be seen as another step in the destruction of the Native cultures along the Columbia River.

Further, as the Grand Coulee Dam lacks a fish ladder, fish migration, critical to Natives and others, was permanently blocked. The Spokane and other Native tribes were prevented from holding traditional salmon ceremonies as the spawning grounds became extinct. The various types of salmon, including Chinook, steelhead, sockeye and coho, in addition to other fish species such as the lamprey, are unable to spawn in the reaches of the Upper Columbia Basin.

As he had for the work on the Bonneville Dam, folk singer Woody Guthrie wrote and sang several famous songs about the Grand Coulee Dam, including 1941's "Roll On, Columbia, Roll On" and "Grand Coulee Dam" of the same year. Guthrie had been commissioned by the Bonneville Power Administration to write the songs in conjunction with a documentary movie project about the dam. The songs praised the public works projects that arose out of President Franklin Delano Roosevelt's New Deal that helped lift America out of the Great Depression. The New Deal consisted of programs, public work projects, financial regulations and other reforms during the period from 1933 to 1939. The songs describe the power of the Columbia River, the wildness of the setting, the Lewis and Clark Expedition of the early nineteenth century, the bravery and difficult work performed by the construction crews and the deaths that occurred and the power harnessing the river provided. "Roll On, Columbia, Roll On" was adopted in 1987 as the official folk song of Washington State. The state legislature, in adopting the song, said, "The Columbia River is the pride of the northwest and the unifying geographic element of the state."

CHAPTER 22

WALLA WALLA, WASHINGTON

The Whitman Killings

F ort Nez Perce (French for "pierced nose") was established in 1818 by the Northwest Company to trade with the local Native people. It became a major stop for migrants into the Oregon Country. The fort was renamed Fort Walla Walla (the area is adjacent to the Walla Walla River, where it adjoins the Columbia River) and became a U.S. Army outpost in 1856. Walla Walla was incorporated in 1862 and grew rapidly due to the gold rush in Idaho. The city is now the largest in Walla Walla County, Washington, in the southeastern part of the state, with an estimated population of thirty-three thousand. Walla Walla is the county seat, and the main industry is agriculture.

Physician Marcus Whitman and his wife, Narcissa, arrived in the area on September 1, 1836, and established the Whitman Mission to try to convert the local Walla Walla Native population to Christianity. The Whitmans were murdered on November 29, 1847, and their deaths have resulted in purported hauntings in the area.

Marcus Whitman practiced medicine in Canada and New York. He offered his services to the American Board of Commissioners for Foreign Missions and visited the Oregon Territory, where he found the Flathead, Nez Perce and other Natives to be friendly. He later returned to the West with his new wife, Narcissa. The Whitmans were accompanied by the Reverend Henry H. Spalding; his wife, Eliza; and two single men. Narcissa Whitman and Eliza Spalding were the first white women to cross the Continental Divide. Whitman founded a mission among the Cayuse at Waiilatpu, six miles west of

Above: A Walla Walla, Washington park, 2017. *Courtesy of wwboy, Pixabay.*

Opposite: Walla Walla, Washington barns, 2018. *Courtesy of RainWater Gallery, Pixabay.*

present-day Walla Walla. He helped the Natives build houses, till their fields, irrigate their crops and erect mills for grinding corn and wheat. Narcissa established a mission school. Progress was slow, and Whitman found the Natives to be apathetic. The Natives were attracted to the ceremonial form of worship conducted by Roman Catholic missionaries. A competition for their conversion ensued.

Whitman's task was complicated by the influence of lawless white newcomers. Sensing the Natives' growing dissatisfaction with him, Whitman decided to relocate his family. However, before he was able to do so, an epidemic of measles broke out among the whites and Natives. Whitman cared for the suffering, but while many of the white children recovered, many of the Natives (lacking immunity) did not. The Natives suspected Whitman of practicing sorcery in order to remove the Natives to make way for more white settlers. On November 29, 1847, the Natives attacked, killing fourteen white people, including the Whitmans, and kidnapping fifty-three women and children. Termed the Whitman Massacre, this event called the nation's attention to the difficulties faced by settlers in the far western United States. This contributed to early passage of a bill to organize the Oregon Territory in 1848. It also led directly to the Cayuse War, an armed conflict between the U.S. government and white settlers versus the local Natives. This war did not end until 1850, followed by the Cayuse tribe handing over five members

for the Whitman murders (Tilaukaikt, Tomahas, Klokamas, Isaiachalkis and Kimasumpkin). These five men were hanged on June 3, 1850, after being convicted by a military commission.

As we have seen, tragedies like the Whitman Massacre and the Cayuse War tend to be associated with increased paranormal activity. These types of events scar the land and environment and are said to have supernatural ramifications.

A number of sites of the Cayuse War are said to be haunted. Witnesses have reported hearing pounding horse hooves, as if the animals are being ridden by ghostly soldiers and Natives.

The Phi Delt House at Whitman College, named in honor of the slain Dr. Whitman and his wife, is said to be haunted by a former house member, nicknamed the "Blue Man." A second-floor bedroom near the south end of the house has been the site of these hauntings.

The Whitmans' contributions are commemorated at the Whitman Mission National Historic Site near Walla Walla.

CHAPTER **23**

LA GRANDE, BAKER CITY AND MALHEUR BUTTE, OREGON

Hot Lake, Ghostly Geiser Grand Hotel and Witches

L a Grande, Oregon, is located to the south of Walla Walla, Washington, and to the southeast of the Columbia River. Originally named Brownsville, it is the county seat of Union County. It was a waypoint along the Oregon Trail and was first settled by white immigrants in 1861. The Hot Lake Hotel dates back to 1864. It partially burned down in 1934 and then served as a World War II–era nurses' training school. Later, it served as an insane asylum. In 1979, it was placed in the National Register of Historic Places. It is also known as one of the most haunted places in Oregon. Visitors report strange, shadowy figures walking the hotel's grounds late at night. They also report strange, unexplainable disembodied voices and footsteps. Some staff believe these emanate from former guests of the hotel. Others believe the voices and footsteps may belong to the ghosts of people who died by suicide at the asylum. The hotel was renovated in 2003. Also in La Grande, the spirit of a woman said to have been killed in Candy Cane Park was observed making a merry-go-round spin uncontrollably fast at a now-defunct carnival. It is now said she haunts the park benches.

Baker City, Oregon, is also located to the south of Walla Walla. The city was incorporated in 1874 and was named in honor of U.S. senator Edward D. Baker, the only sitting U.S. senator killed in military conflict. He died in 1861, leading a charge of Union soldiers during the Civil War. The Geiser Grand Hotel, first called the Hotel Warshauer, founded in 1889, is striking with its ornately carved mahogany columns, Victorian-style chandeliers and stained glass. *Sunset Magazine* said there is "no finer hotel between Salt Lake

City and Portland." The *New York Times* said it is a "sparkling symbol of the gold-mining boom." *Newsweek* included it in its story about the "unique hotels of the world," and *Fodor's Travel Guide* described it as "opulent." First built for wealthy 1880s miners, the hotel fell into disrepair in the 1960s. It was restored in the 1990s, and employees and guests have described strange and eerie sounds, a sense of paranormal activities and a number of ghosts.

These spirits include a young girl, a 1920s saloon dancer or flapper, a woman in a 1930s-era purple dress, a headless chef and a cowboy and his girlfriend. The hotel is thought of by some as one of the most haunted places in Oregon. Some guests have reported being awakened by the smell of cherry cigar smoke being blown into their faces, room doors being sometimes difficult to open and feeling cold spots in their rooms, fingers tightening around their throats, temperature drops of up to thirty degrees (and being able to see one's breath) and pain in the head and body. One job interviewee described feeling like someone was standing behind them, breathing on them and then pushing them, but there was no one there. One of the hotel's best-known apparitions is the Lady in Blue, who is thought to be named Annabelle and is sometimes seen walking or floating up and down the main staircase wearing a long blue gown. Further, a former hotel owner named Maybelle Geiser lived in room 302, and that room is said to be filled with paranormal activity, jewelry that rearranges itself and disappearing complimentary snacks. The hotel offers ghost tours several times a year.

To the south of Baker City is Malheur Butte, Oregon. The butte is a dormant volcano, and the name Malheur is French for "evil hour." It is reputed to be a spot where a coven of witches formerly met. Residents believe the witches will return and have left their shadows behind to protect the area from those encroaching upon it. The spirits of small dogs have been seen protecting the area. Hikers and visitors have reported being chased away by "menacing, shadowy creatures that screech."

Chapter 24
Spokane, Washington

Spooks Along the River

The city of Spokane sits along the Spokane River, north of the Snake River. The first people in this area were members of the Spokane Native tribe. A European trading post was established here in 1810. The Northern Pacific Railway was completed in 1881 and brought in settlers, and the city was incorporated that same year as Spokane Falls; it was shortened to Spokane ten years later. Silver and gold were discovered here in the late 1800s.

The morgue (a term common among newspapers to describe their paper archives) of the *Spokesman-Review* (Spokane's more than 135-year-old newspaper)—a windowless, dark and rarely visited room—lies in the basement of the Review Tower. The morgue holds stacks of yellowing paper, and some say the eyes of long-dead Spokanites stare out from the paper and voices from the past can be heard. The numerous file cabinets contain stories of death, murder and missing people. Thousands of envelopes contain hundreds of articles and stories about ghosts, witches, sea serpents and monsters. I discuss some of these stories in the following paragraphs.

The elegant Davenport Hotel was built in the early 1900s by Louis Davenport. It is said that the Davenport lobby has a ghost story to tell. It was August 17, 1920, nearing 7:00 p.m., and the lobby was filled with those waiting to dine. The stately main hotel dining room was filled with the sounds of conversation and silverware being handled. One hotel guest, Ellen McNamara, sixty-eight, a rich widow from New York City, was traveling with her sister and two cousins through the western United States. Their

The clock tower in Spokane, Washington, 2015. *Courtesy of shawnaller, Pixabay.*

next stop was to be Glacier National Park in Montana, but McNamara wasn't feeling well. As they sat in the Isabella Room (the Davenport's original dining room, now a ballroom), McNamara stood, walked to a door, opened it and inexplicably stepped onto the third-floor glass skylight. The skylight, unable to hold her weight, gave way, and she tumbled into the lobby below her, near the entrance to Sprague Avenue. The sound of breaking glass permeated the dining room, cutting sharply through the noise of guests being served and eating dinner. Approximately one hundred people present in the dining room saw her fall. Witnesses say her "shoulder struck the floor first and…her head crashed against the stone." Some men carried her to a couch, and still conscious, she was reported to have said her final words: "Where did I go?" She became "insensible" (meaning to have lost one's mental faculties), was taken to her room and died within the hour. Over the years, people have debated whether Ellen's death was an accident or suicide. Guests have reported seeing, once or twice a week, the spirit of a woman dressed in 1920s attire, presumably McNamara, leaning over the railing above the lobby, looking for someone but never saying a word. Her spirit is said to scream for several minutes before disappearing.

In the winter of 1934, a figure draped in a sheet was reported to be terrorizing the people of East Central Spokane, then called Union Park. This figure was described as a wraithlike (pale and thin) creature, called the "ghost of Union Park," and was said to have frightened children, peeped into windows and roamed the city's streets at night. The police said the ghost seemed to disappear when they approached it, leaving no footprints. A local woman came forward and identified the ghost as her son, who was a traumatized war veteran. She promised to keep him home at night, and the story faded from the newspapers. Some still believed the ghost was something more than what the soldier's mother said.

Sea monsters have also been reported in the area. A local man named M.L. Little wrote a letter to the local editor on August 27, 1944, reporting a sea serpent in Omak Lake. Omak Lake is the largest saline or salt-based lake in Washington State. Little was traveling with his friend Fred Howard and said he saw two large, long logs lying close to shore. However, seconds later, Miller said one of these logs seemed to be swinging around and heading out into the lake. The logs were each twelve to sixteen feet long, two feet in diameter and submerged just under the water's surface. Little wrote, "The rough blotch of the body remained quite visible and the water in turmoil during its passage." Little said the creature's head, the size of a thirty-gallon drum, broke the water's surface several times. He said the men "easily followed its progress the entire distance to the cliffs at the far end of the lake where it splashed for a very few seconds, then disappeared from view."

No other sightings were reported, and the story dissipated from the news. However, a decade later, on May 15, 1956, C.F. Dement wrote another letter to the editor. In this, Dement described the "monster of Rock Lake," a deep, cliff-lined lake in the Scablands of Washington not far from Omak Lake. He said local Natives had historically stayed away from the lake because it was home to a monster. He also talked about how a local landowner told him she had seen something huge, as big as a tree, on top of the water suddenly splash and go under. The source of these stories has never been found.

The Monroe Street Bridge opened in 1911 and was, at the time, the biggest concrete arch bridge in America. It has been renovated several times, in 1925, 1934 and 2003. There have been reports the bridge is haunted by the spirit of a construction worker killed during the construction of a smaller bridge that stood in the same spot, before the current one. Witnesses have said he is dressed in old-fashioned clothing and asks where all the Natives have gone. When approached, it is said he throws himself off the bridge, toward the water below, but disappears before he hits the water.

A Spokane, Washington bridge, 2021. *Courtesy of carriedugovic, Pixabay.*

Greenwood Cemetery has been described as "creepy." Steps leading down to the cemetery were built but then abandoned due to a rumor that spirits were seen blocking any visitors deemed "unworthy" of entering. An alternative entrance was created, although some brave souls still attempt to enter the cemetery by way of the steps.

Built in 1931 for the huge sum of $1 million, Spokane's Fox Theater is described as lovely. The Fox fell into disrepair over the decades but was renovated recently at a price of approximately $30 million. It is said the original architect, Robert Reamer, haunts the theater to this day. Witnesses have reported seeing him wandering the building, inspecting various features.

The Patsy Clark Mansion, built in 1897 as a private residence for a millionaire, currently houses a local law firm. Reports indicate the original owners are still present, throwing parties and playing music. Witnesses have reported seeing a ghost named Mary, dressed in old-fashioned party clothes, walking down a staircase.

Spokane was the site of brutal conflicts between the Natives and early settlers. The Natives are said to have killed many settlers for encroaching on their land. To retaliate against the Natives' attacks, in 1858, settlers were said to have slaughtered some eight hundred Spokane horses, on which the Natives relied. To this day, witnesses have reported seeing dozens of ghostly horses in the area.

In the 1920s and 1930s, the Hahn Mansion was the home of playboy millionaire Rudolph Hahn. It is said that in 1940, Hahn's lover was found dead in the house, and although it was ruled a suicide, some believed Hahn had murdered her. He moved away soon after and was himself murdered by a salesman. Witnesses have reported the mansion is haunted by Hahn's dead lover.

In 1898, pioneer James Monaghan built a private mansion for him and his family. In 1942, the mansion was renamed Monaghan Hall and made part of Gonzaga University. The university's music conservatory is housed in the building, and in the 1970s, there were reportedly many inexplicable disturbances. These include a door handle turning on its own before the door was flung open with force, the organ playing itself, growling coming from a locked storage room, flute music playing in an empty music room and even security guards being strangled. In 1975, an exorcism was performed of the building, but students have continued to express an uneasiness in entering it.

The modern Mirabeau Park Hotel is said to be one of the most haunted locations in Spokane. Witnesses have reported paintings being pushed off walls, doors and windows being slammed shut on their own, items moving around and being pushed up and down the stairs.

In 1927, a man named R.J. Mourning died a mysterious death in the town of Fairfield, southeast of Spokane. Some stories hold that Mourning died after falling out of a barn loft, while others said he fell out of a moving car. The *Spokane Daily Chronicle* headline read "Death Followed a Drunken Debauch." Mourning's family began to report seeing a ghost in a deep ravine where he could not have escaped, but he finally vanished in thin air. The family reported other odd events, including another spirit leading a team of horses that was pulling a car out of a field. They reported seeing another ghost back up a car directly at their house. They observed odd marks on the floor of a deserted house, rockets being fired from a nearby hill, flashes of light in the night and a man making mysterious appearances and disappearances. These family reports prompted a nearby prosecutor named Greenough to reopen a murder investigation. On October 27, 1927, the *Chronicle* reported that a ghost had been seen in Fairfield; some citizens believed Mourning had met a violent death and his ghost was calling for vengeance. The prosecutor was quoted as saying, "Some think they have seen the ghost and I have been looking for material evidence, but I am at a loss to know just what happened."

The case has remained a mystery, but local sheriff deputies have indicated their belief that "liquor runners" using a deserted building were found by R.J. Mourning, and they were the cause of his death. The *Spokane Daily Chronicle* reported the deputies "have been hot on the trail of the ghosts, but they are inclined to believe that moonshiners and not phantoms are back of the strange manifestations."

Spokane, Washington, has no shortage of haunted and ghostly tales.

CHAPTER 25

PALOUSE, WASHINGTON

St. Ignatius Hospital Hauntings

I t is thought the name "Palouse" comes from the Palus Native American tribe. Palouse is defined by fertile hills and prairies that lie north of the Snake River. It boomed in the 1880s with wheat growing and other agriculture.

Abandoned but not forgotten, St. Ignatius Hospital provided healthcare to the Palouse region from 1893 to 1964. In 1892, Reverend Jachern, a Roman Catholic priest, recognized the need for improved healthcare in the area. He traveled to Portland, Oregon, and invited the Sisters of Charity to build a hospital in Palouse. In order to build hospitals, religious orders across the United States relied on private donations or sponsors for funding. Colfax, Pullman and Palouse City all made competitive offers for the new hospital to be built in their town. With an offer of free water, land, an interest-free loan of $3,000 and another $5,000 promised from the chamber of commerce, the town of Colfax won the bid.

Construction of St. Ignatius Hospital began on April 17, 1893, while three Sisters of Charity provided care in a wooden building located on the site. Their first patient was treated for pneumonia. The new hospital was completed in 1894 and opened that same year. Additions were added in 1917 and 1928. In 1911, the St. Ignatius School of Nursing started and graduated its first class of nurses. By 1936, a separate dormitory for nursing students was opened. Washington State's first two male nurses, Philip Kromm and Archie McClintic, earned their nursing degree from St. Ignatius School of Nursing in 1941.

A Palouse, Washington prairie, 2020. *Courtesy of Designtek, Pixabay.*

An early twentieth-century hospital scene, 1918. *Courtesy of Bain News Service, Pixabay.*

Without government assistance and relying on donations and what patients could afford to pay, it was difficult for St. Ignatius to make needed upgrades. The Sisters of Charity were unable to keep up with the expense of maintaining and modernizing the hospital. In 1964, in the face of a declining population and the desire for a new facility, the state closed St. Ignatius. The former St. Ignatius Hospital became an assisted living facility until it was closed in 2000. In 2015, the Washington Trust for Historic Preservation added St. Ignatius Hospital to its 2015 Most Endangered Properties list.

It has been reported that ghosts of former patients now roam the halls of St. Ignatius Hospital. One of these encounters has been described as a "vicious attack by a huge, black mass." Every October, small groups of people gather with flashlights and ghost-hunting supplies for the annual St. Ignatius Haunted Hospital Tour. F.E. Martin, the hospital's first fatality, died in 1893, crushed to death between two railroad cars. His restless spirit reportedly haunts the halls of St. Ignatius Hospital. Filmmakers also visit the hospital in search of ghosts. Despite the hauntings, St. Ignatius Hospital is vacant and in serious need of renovation. Efforts are underway to save not only a piece of Colfax's history but also the history of frontier healthcare in the United States.

St. Ignatius Hospital has been featured on the Travel Channel show *Ghost Adventures*.

CHAPTER 26

CLARKSTON, WASHINGTON, AND LEWISTON, IDAHO

Jawbone Flats

C larkston, Washington, on the Snake River was named for Captain William Clark of the Lewis and Clark Expedition, which passed by the area in canoes in 1805. It was first settled by white people in 1862 and officially incorporated in 1902. It went by various names—Jawbone Flats, Lewiston and Concord—before receiving its current name.

Directly across the Snake River from Clarkston is Lewiston, Idaho, named for Captain Meriwether Lewis of the Lewis and Clark Expedition. Lewiston is the ninth-largest city in Idaho, with approximately thirty-two thousand residents. It is located at the confluence of the Snake and Clearwater Rivers. The city was founded in 1861 in the wake of a gold rush and named the capital of the newly established Idaho Territory, until Boise was named the capital in 1864.

Numerous hauntings have been reported in the area. In 2015, a dishwasher at Brava's and Brock's restaurant and bar in downtown Lewiston reported hearing his name being said by a disembodied voice and feeling cold spots. On one occasion, he said he witnessed an apparition of a woman with short hair sitting at the Brock's bar after closing. Earlier that evening, he indicated he and his manager heard a disembodied voice saying his name. As a dishwasher, he was normally the last person to leave the bar. He said he was making sure everything was prepared for opening the next morning when he noticed a wine glass sitting on the bar, which he then cleaned. While returning the glass, he noticed two more were set in the same spot as

A Lewiston, Idaho river, 2020. *Courtesy of jdblack, Pixabay.*

the previous glass. After cleaning the glasses, he decided to call it a night. The dishwasher said that at the end of his six months of employment at Brava's, the wine glass scenario had repeated itself four times. Under the restaurant are Lewiston's underground tunnels and passageways, which have also experienced hauntings. Some locals say the tunnels were built during excavation or for sewer access and may have been used to deliver goods without needing to walk the greater distance above ground.

In the 1980s, two young women who were visiting the Lewiston Civic Theatre, as well as a male theater employee, disappeared one night. The young women's bodies were found a distance away, while the man's body has never been found. Police indicated they believed a second male employee working at the theater at the time was responsible, but they could not secure sufficient evidence. The missing employee's family believes his body is buried somewhere on the theater grounds, but they have been unsuccessful in gaining authorization to search. These events have led to speculation that the theater is haunted, with reports of the spirits of a young girl as well as up to dozens of other ghosts.

Residents of Lake Waha have reported observing the spirit of a Native American woman walking around the lake's shore. They reported that she disappears when seen, creating a whirlpool in the lake as this happens.

Clarkston, Washington, 2019. *Courtesy of jdblack, Pixabay.*

The Lewiston Clarkston Paranormal Research Society has indicated there are numerous ghosts that call the area home. They have searched the area for spirits with voice recorders, cameras, flashlights, electromagnetic (EMF) meters and a ghost box. They reported strange energy emanating from cemeteries and other locations.

Oregon's Hells Canyon, through which the Snake River flows, got its name in 1895 from the earliest white settlers, possibly due to its dark canyon walls. The settlers had tried to tame the Snake River by navigating their boats and ferries down it, but they were generally unsuccessful. Hells Canyon is ten miles wide at its widest point and appears to hold a dark secret. In May 1887, thirty-four Chinese gold miners were massacred. Chinese gold miners, under the leadership of Chea Po and Lee She, left Lewiston up the Snake River in October 1886. A gang led by Bruce Evans, nicknamed "Old Blue," ambushed and robbed the Chinese miners of between $4,000 and $50,000 in gold, murdered them and then mutilated the miners' bodies. Reports at the time described the massacre as "brutal," with the gang wrecking and burning the camp and throwing the miners' mutilated corpses into the Snake River. Some dead miners' bodies washed ashore, while others were not found for months or, in some cases, years. One of the members of the gang made a deathbed confession to his father, which was published in 1891. He described the gang shooting the miners and in one case "beating the brains out" of one of the miners over a several-day period. A grand jury indictment and trial were conducted. From the evidence, it appeared the massacre was premeditated and was, in part, to eliminate the Chinese miners from the area. One federal law enforcement official, J.K. Vincent, said "everyone was shot, cut up and stripped and thrown in the River." A newspaper article published on July 1, 1887, in the *Lebanon Express* called the corpses a "severe warning to Chinese miners.…More than likely, it was the whites who look with an evil eye upon Chinese intrusion in American mines. The American miner kicks hard at the Chinese miner."

A July 17, 1887 *San Bernardino Daily Courier* article titled "Chinese Not Killed by Whites" indicated the Chinese miners had been murdered by rival Chinese miners, as the massacre victims were "shot in the back and mutilated by cleavers, a weapon in general use by the Chinese."

Despite the deathbed and one other confession, the gang members received little or no punishment for their crime. Some of the gang members fled America, while the three members tried by a jury were found not guilty. The name of the leader of the gang—Bruce Evans—is engraved on the Enterprise, Oregon courthouse square memorial arch, honoring him as an early pioneer.

The U.S. Board on Geographic Names officially renamed the area the "Chinese Massacre Cove" in 2005 to honor the dead, and a plaque was placed there in 2012 with an inscription in Chinese, English and the Native language of the Nez Perce. A 2010 book by William Howarth and Anne Mathews, titled *Deep Creek*, offered a fictionalized account of the massacre. It was selected as one of 2010's best novels by the *Washington Post*.

The Clarkston and Lewis area, named for the explorers Lewis and Clark, certainly has more than its fair share of haunted legends and ghostly tales.

EPILOGUE

This completes our journey along the Columbia River, other waterways and nearby areas. I hope you found it as interesting to read about as I found it to research and write about. I am fascinated by the Pacific Northwest's history and culture. It was one of the last parts of the United States to be explored and settled, making it seem more "wild" than other parts of the country.

There is no better way to discover the beauty and history of the Pacific Northwest than to explore the Pacific coast, the rivers and the towns near their shores. Rustic riverfront villages, restaurants, antique stores, surf shops and carnivals abound, while farmers' markets and weekly tourist festivals welcome residents and visitors alike. The area is known for great hiking, boating, camping, fishing, biking, clamming, golfing, cranberry cultivation, oyster farming and tourism activities, while state parks with nineteenth-century military forts and national historic sites welcome history enthusiasts. Bald eagles, black bears, elk, deer and other wildlife call the area home, and gray whales can be spotted in the Pacific, migrating twice a year.

The daring exploits of frontiersmen and adventurers took place on these waterways. The rivers offer dramatic scenery as they follow the path of the famed 1805 and 1806 Lewis and Clark Corps of Discovery. The diverse panorama of environments and history ranges from the lush beauty of the Pacific coast to the dramatic eruption of Mount St. Helens, to the spectacular scenery of the Columbia River Gorge and the Snake River's Hells Canyon. Through locks and dams, the rivers flow and the distant horizon and snow-capped mountains seem to touch the sky.

While the Pacific Northwest offers breathtaking scenery and an idyllic setting, it has also been identified as one of the most haunted regions in the United States. In this book, I examined reported hauntings, folkloric tales and supernatural creatures said to inhabit the areas along and near the Columbia and Snake Rivers, tributaries from Oregon and Washington to the Idaho border and nearby coastal areas.

The spirits of the Natives, frontiersmen, adventurers, boatmen and early settlers seem to cling to the rivers, lakes, shores and towns. Inland nautical disasters have claimed many lives, and reported paranormal activity is heavily influenced by nautical legacies and accompanying superstitions. Mariners and passengers have been swallowed by the waters for as long as can be remembered. The spirits of sailors and passengers who suffered these dramatic shipwrecks are said to linger. On land, lingering spirits are said to include those of early settlers perhaps wishing to remain close to their homes and descendants or to complete unfinished business; Native Americans whose lands were stolen and burial grounds desecrated; murderers and murder victims; and soldiers. In addition to these ghost stories, there are countless tales of sea serpents, Bigfoot, Thunderbirds and other supernatural creatures. Chilling tales of paranormal occurrences abound in this northwestern corner of America.

The dark skies, wind, storms and fog all add to an atmosphere of mystery and dread. Damaging storms and other natural events, as well as those that are man-made, can have a dramatic effect on towns and waterways. We discussed the region's folklore, nautical superstitions, ghosts and the undead and supernatural creatures.

We have explored many areas in this book, from Oregon, to Washington, to the Idaho border. We visited cities such as Astoria, Oregon, the first American settlement west of the Rocky Mountains; and Portland, Oregon, regularly rated as one of the most haunted cities in America. We sailed on the Columbia River, nicknamed the "river of floaters" for the many dead bodies found in it. We journeyed along the Oregon Trail, where some thirty-four thousand settlers and adventurers suffered and are said to have died. We discussed wrecked ships, snowbound trains, hijackings and airline crashes. We focused on mighty dams, which created much-needed energy but also claimed numerous workers' lives and displaced Native peoples. Wherever we have journeyed, we have found fascinating folklore, tales and stories.

I encourage you to visit and explore this beautiful part of America, and remember, wherever you journey, safe travels!

Bibliography

Abbot, C. "Rajneeshees." Oregon Encyclopedia, March 17, 2018.

Addis, C. "Whitman Killings." Oregon Encyclopedia, February 9, 2021.

Anderson, J. "Oregon's Haunted Spots." *Travel Oregon*, September 28, 2016.

Atlas Obscura. "The Witch's Castle." February 10, 2016.

Baker, M. "FBI Has Chased Hundreds of D.B. Cooper Ghosts." KOMO News, Associated Press, August 4, 2011.

Beach Connection. "What Ghosts Gather around Fort Stevens." Beachconnection.net.

Bureau of Reclamation. "Columbia-Pacific Northwest Region."

Callum, S. "Rogue Ales Public House." Hauntedplaces.org.

Campuzano, E. "Oregon Ghost Stories: 31 Famous Haunted Places." Oregonlive.com, October 22, 2016.

Carey, B. "Gigantic Apes Coexisted with Early Humans, Study Finds." LIVESCIENCE, November 7, 2005.

CBS News. "Alleged D.B. Cooper DNA Not a Match." August 8, 2011.

Chong, R. "The Forgotten Chinese Massacre at Hells Canyon." AsAm News, September 14, 2020. asamnews.com.

Cray, L. "Trapped in the Columbia Gorge: Documenting a Train Rescue during the Great Winter Storm of 1884–1885." Oregon Historical Society, December 15, 2020.

Danko, M. "25 Facts about Stanley Kubrick's *The Shining*." Mentalfloss.com, October 28, 2018.

Davis, J., and A. Eufrasio. *Weird Washington: Your Travel Guide to Washington's Local Legends and Best Kept Secrets*. N.p.: Sterling, 2008.

Denham, D. "12 Haunted Pacific Northwest Trails and Places Where Horror Lurks." *That Oregon Life*, October 12, 2021.

Deshais, N. "Haunted Tales of Spokane's Past Fill Newspaper Morgue." *Spokesman-Review*, October 31, 2018.

Duncan-Strong, W. "The Occurrence and Wider Implications of a 'Ghost Cult' on the Columbia River Suggested by Carvings in Wood, Bone and Stone." Literary Licensing, LLC, *Oregonian* newspaper, September 9, 1896.

Education World. "Oregon Trail." educationworld.com.

Encyclopedia Britannica. "Marcus Whitman, American Missionary." January 6, 2021.

Everything Explained. "Grand Coulee Dam Explained." Everythingexplained. com.

Fahrenbach, W. Bigfoot Researchers Organization, December 6, 1975, and February 1993.

Farrell Realty. "Haunted Places in North Portland." farrellrealty.com/blog. 2016.

Finn, J. "'Colossal Claude,' the Great Columbia Sea Serpent." Offbeat Oregon History, February 4, 2020.

Free Horror. "The Boy Ghost of the Columbia River Haunts the Banks of Kennewick." Freehorror.net.

Ghosts of America. "Leavenworth, Washington Ghost Sightings." GhostsofAmerica.com.

Guthrie, Woody. "Grand Coulee Dam."

———. "Jackhammer Blues."

———. "Roll On, Columbia."

Hanauer, E. "Seafaring Superstitions & Marine Myth Rituals Explored." *Dive Training*, 2006.

Hanover, D. "Seafaring Superstitions & Marine Myth Rituals Explained." *Dive Training*, August 6, 2006.

Haunted Places. "Haunted Places in Kamiah, Idaho." Hauntedplaces.org.

———. "Haunted Places in Umatilla, Oregon." Hauntedplaces.org.

———. "Lewiston Civic Theatre." Hauntedplaces.com.

Haunted Rooms. "Most Haunted Places in Spokane, WA." Hauntedrooms. com.

Hayden Island Bridge Cam. i5bridgecam.wordpress.com.

The Historic Sunset Highway. "The Historic Sunset Highway in Washington-Govan." Road-warrior@sunset-hwy.com.

Historic Tours of America. "Types of Ghosts." historictours.com.

John, Finn J.D. "Graveyard of the Oregon Trail Still Said to Be Haunted." Offbeat Oregon History, August 24, 2009. offbeatoregon.com.

Lafferty, K. "Ghost Hunt with the Lewiston Clarkston Paranormal Research Society." KLEW, 2016. klewtv.com.

Lebanon Express, July 1, 1887.

Legends of America. "Disease and Death on the Overland Trails." www.legendsofamerica.com.

Levine, D. "Ghost Adventures Encounters an 'Unholy' Presence at Haunted Hotel." Popculture.com, October 13, 2018.

Llacqua, J. "Sasquatch and the Law: The Implications of Bigfoot Preservation Laws in Washington State." HGSA Conference Paper, 2014.

The Making of America. National Geographic Society, 2002.

McCorkle, B. "Paranormal Investigators Scour Longview Mansion for Signs of the Supernatural." *Daily News*, October 22, 2011.

McKee, T. "The Conductor: A Richland County Ghost Story." RichlandSource, 2020.

Moller, N. "Starvation Creek." Oregon Encyclopedia, March 17, 2018.

Munger, S. "Ghosts of Conventions Past: A Portland Hotel's Checkered History." September 16, 2016.

National Historic Oregon Trail Interpretive Center. "History Bits & Westward Quotes on the Oregon Trail." oregontrail.blm.gov.

Northeast Oregon Now. "A Haunting in Umatilla." August 12, 2013.

O'Neill, N. "Nearly Every Week, a Body Is Found in a Portland River. This Is Not Normal." *Willamette Week*, September 13, 2017.

Only in Your State. "The Creepy Small Town in Oregon with Insane Paranormal Activity."

———. "The Historic Geiser Grand Hotel in Oregon Is Notoriously Haunted and We Dare You to Spend the Night." onlyinyourstate.com.

Oregon Haunted Houses. "Geiser Grand Hotel—Real Haunt in Baker City, Oregon." Oregonhauntedhouses.com.

Oregon Journal. "Bunko Kelly Pardoned after Thirteen Years." July 21, 1907.

Ostler, J. *Surviving Genocide: Native Nations and United States from the American Revolution to Bleeding Kansas*. New Haven, CT: Yale University Press, 2019.

Perry, D. "1978 Plane Crash into Portland Neighborhood Killed 10, Allowed a Prisoner Escape—and Haunted Pilot." *Oregonian*, August 29, 2019.

Portland Ghosts. "The Crystal Ballroom."

———. "The Heathman Hotel." portlandghosts.com.

———. "Most Haunted Places in Oregon." portlandghosts.com.

———. "The Pittock Mansion." portlandghosts.com.

Puzzle Box Horror. "Hood River Oregon's Haunted Hotels." September 7, 2020. puzzleboxhorror.com.

Ramirez, D. "Bonneville Dam—Admire Wonders of Engineering and Mitigating Salmon at This Historic Landmark on the Columbia River." Travelportland.com, June 11, 2021.

Richardson, T. "Spirit Lurks in Richland Restaurant." *Tri-City Herald*, October 29, 2015.

Rideout, J. "Got Ghosts." *Astorian*, September 30, 2008.

Run of the River Inn & Refuge. "Ghost Towns and Haunted Places in the Washington Cascades." runoftheriver.com.

San Bernardino Daily Courier. "Chinese Not Killed by Whites." July 17, 1887.

Sasquatch Chronicles. April 5, 2019. sasquatchchronicles.com.

Sauthoff, P. "Tim Moreau Would Have Been 50 This Month, Had He Not Been the Victim of One of Portland's Most Remarkable Crime Stories." *Willamette Week*, May 22, 2018.

Schultz, R. "St. Ignatious Hospital—A Haunted Hospital in the Palouse?" Spokane Historical Organization, 2021.

Seattle Times. "FBI Kills Man in Threat to Bonneville Dam." October 21, 1996.

Snider, P. "Ghosts in the Gorge." Northwest50Plus, 2016.

Southwick, N. "Coyote Stories: A Salishan Trickster." Spokane Historical, SpokaneHistorical.org, 2021.

Steelmantown Cemetery Company. "Historic Columbian Cemetery Portland, Oregon." destinationdestinymemorials.com/services/natural-burial/columbian-cemetery.

Stewart, D. "Is the Bagdad Theatre in Portland Haunted?" America's Haunted Road Trip, August 8, 2017.

Travel Channel. "The Lewis and Clark Conspiracy." *Lost Secrets*, season 1, episode 5.

Triezenberg, J. "The North Coast's Legendary Sea Monsters." *Astorian*, October 9, 2020.

Tsur, H. "Ghosts in the Grove." *Preserving Forest Grove* (newsletter of the Historic Landmarks Board), Fall 2009.

U.S. Bureau of Land Management (BLM). "History Bits and Westward Quotes." N.d.

Wang, A. "Cathedral Park Is among the Stops in 'Ghostland,' a Tour of Haunted Places." *Oregonian*, October 7, 2016.

———. "Severed Feet—Still Inside Shoes—Keep Mysteriously Washing Up on Pacific Northwest Shores." *Washington Post*, February 11, 2016.

The Weird U.S. "The Thunderbird." weirdus.com.

Winters, M. "Is It Time to Pull the Oldest Profession Out in the Sunshine?" *Astorian*, May 29, 2014.

Wood, M. "The Most Haunted Hotels in the World." *USA Today*, October 30, 2014.

ABOUT THE AUTHOR

I ra Wesley Kitmacher is an author, professor, attorney, public speaker and retired senior federal executive. Originally from Massachusetts, he has lived in California, Nevada, Virginia and now Washington State. Ira retired in 2019 as a senior federal executive after thirty-six years. He also served as a professor, teaching graduate and undergraduate-level courses for Georgetown University in Washington, D.C.; Portland State University in Oregon; Grays Harbor College in Aberdeen, Washington; and Clatsop Community College in Astoria, Oregon.

Ira is fascinated by the history of the American Pacific Northwest, especially the Columbia and Snake Rivers. In addition to writing this and other books, he regularly appears on radio and podcasts, in newspapers and as a public speaker at conferences. He has designed and is teaching a course in Astoria, Oregon, on haunted Pacific Northwest folklore. He has also developed and is leading haunted and history tours of Washington's Long Beach Peninsula. He lives in the area with his wife, Wendy; their two children, David and Gabi (when they come to visit); and three dogs.

He hopes you enjoy this journey along the Columbia and Snake Rivers, other tributaries and the nearby coastal and land areas as much as he enjoyed researching and writing about it.

Visit us at
www.historypress.com